THE NATIONAL WILDLIFE FEDERATION'S GUIDE TO

GARDENING
FOR
WILDLIFE

THE NATIONAL WILDLIFE FEDERATION'S GUIDE TO

GARDENING
FOR
WILDLIFE

How to Create a Beautiful Backyard Habitat for Birds, Butterflies and Other Wildlife

CRAIG TUFTS AND PETER LOEWER

RODALE

Rodale Press, Emmaus, Pennsylvania

ROUND STONE PRESS STAFF:
Directors: Marsha Melnick, Susan E. Meyer, Paul Fargis
Developmental Editor: Nick Viorst
General Editor: Anne Halpin
Designer: Jan Melchior
Illustrator: Lauren Jarrett
Production: Don Cooper
Principal Photographer: Jerry Pavia
A complete list of photographers will be found on page 192.

RODALE PRESS STAFF:
Executive Editor, Home and Garden Books: Margaret Lydic Balitas
Senior Editor: Ellen Phillips
Copy Editor: Sarah Dunn
Editor-in-Chief, Rodale Books: William Gottlieb

If you have any questions or comments concerning this book, please write to:
Rodale Press, Inc., Book Readers' Service, 33 East Minor Street, Emmaus, PA 18098

The mission of the National Wildlife Federation is to educate, inspire, and assist individuals and organizations of diverse cultures to conserve wildlife and other natural resources and to protect the Earth's environment in order to achieve a peaceful, equitable and sustainable future.

The National Wildlife Federation is one of the nation's largest, most active, and most respected conservation organizations. NWF is fighting for cleaner water, clearer air, protection of endangered wildlife, and conservation of all our precious natural resources. Membership dues help fund all of these activities as well as education programs and vital research. For membership information, call 1-800-822-9919.

Library of Congress Cataloging-in-Publication Data

Tufts, Craig.
    The National Wildlife Federation's guide to gardening for wildlife: how to create a beautiful
backyard habitat for birds, butterflies, and other wildlife / by Craig Tufts and Peter Loewer.
        p.   cm.
    Includes bibliographical references and index.
    ISBN 0–87596–675–6 hardcover
    1. Gardening to attract wildlife. 2. Wildlife attracting. I. Loewer, H. Peter. II. National
Wildlife Federation. III. Title. IV. Title: Gardening for wildlife.
QL59.T85 1995
639.9'2—dc20   95–5262
                                                          CIP

Distributed in the book trade by St. Martin's Press
Printed and bound in Hong Kong

2 4 6 8 10 9 7 5 3 1 hardcover

Contents

Welcome from the National Wildlife Federation

A few years ago, when our sons were young, my wife and I bought a home in a suburb of Washington, D.C. This community had many attractions: It was safe, conveniently close to work, and had good schools nearby. Yet there was still something missing.

As with most developments around our cities, the house we chose occupied an area that was once farmland and woodland—home to a variety of plants and wildlife. The landscape we acquired was, not surprisingly, mostly grass with some foundation plantings, punctuated with a single flowering crabapple and a pair of grow-in-almost-anything silver maples. The nesting places for birds and small mammals had been cleared away by the builders, as had the wonderful diversity of plants that provided food and cover. Hedgerows of red cedar, flowering dogwood, and staghorn sumac, flanked by a mix of wildflowers and native grasses that included Joe-Pye weed, little bluestem, aster, and tickseed, were the first to disappear on the planners' sketches. Then in a crunch of bulldozer-borne reality they were replaced by a street and utility grid, homogeneous houses, and the basic American planting scheme. In short, both the habitat and the wildlife that depended upon it were gone.

Today, I'm happy to say, the habitat is back, and with it the wildlife has returned. There's not the rich diversity of plants and animals that once carpeted the countryside, but it's surely an improvement over what we started with. Our yard now represents a conscious effort to grow and manage a greater variety of plants than we originally found there. We have planted the yard and garden space around our house with over 300 types of shrubs, trees, flowers, and grasses, all of which meet critical habitat needs for hundreds of creatures we call wildlife. Feeding and nesting birds often visit and may spend much of their lives within our 9,000-square-foot lot. Over 40 types of butterflies fly by, looking for nectar and places where newly hatched caterpillars might find a healthy meal. And our boys are growing up living and interacting with wildlife and understanding firsthand its importance in our world.

Our family is not alone in its efforts to recreate the American wild landscape. Since 1973, the National Wildlife Federation (NWF) has offered information and encouragement to millions of individuals and families who want to invite the natural world back into their lives. Through the NWF's popular Backyard Wildlife Habitat Program, thousands of homeowners all across North America have received official commendations for their efforts. These "backyard naturalists" are often leaders in their communities, providing guidance to others who want to develop ecologically sound landscapes.

Perhaps you have already discovered the advantages of creating landscapes that work with—not against—nature. If you have reduced or discontinued the use of fertilizers and harsh pesticides, produced compost, practiced water conservation, or reintroduced native plants into your garden, you have seen for yourself how beneficial and enjoyable these practices can be. Butterflies may float through your landscape once you provide the right plants for them. Your backyard may now resemble a wilderness preserve, and you may have learned not only which six-legged animals are eating your plants but, also who their predators are and how to encourage them to maintain a balance in your garden.

Whether you are a novice planting your first garden or an experienced gardener looking for a new project, this book will guide you through the process of creating and maintaining a wildlife habitat in your yard. It will also serve as a useful companion as you evaluate, plan, and create your new garden—whether you are reading indoors on a rainy day or shopping at your local garden center for plants and materials.

Introducing wildlife habitat to your landscape may sound challenging at first, but it's actually simple. In all likelihood, elements of habitat are present in your garden now. If you have reduced or eliminated pesticides in your landscape and your choice of plant materials offers nesting places and nourishment, you have no doubt already enjoyed the company of a variety of birds, insects, and small mammals. If you are a water gardener, you may have been pleasantly surprised by the appearance of frogs. Perhaps you have looked out your window on a hot afternoon and seen butterflies at your zinnias or a hummingbird sampling nectar from a patch of salvia or impatiens.

The actual appearance of creatures in the garden is a terrific encouragement to wildlife gardeners. The one comment we hear over and over from gardeners who are just starting out with a wildlife habitat is, "We simply cannot believe how 'alive' our garden has become." One gardener told me that a single clump of an orange-eye butterfly bush planted just the year before had attracted a dozen different types of butterflies one balmy August morning. That same day, her four-year-old daughter saw hummingbirds darting from one nectar plant to another, with long pauses at pineapple sage and trumpet creeper. And after this gardener added a small pond lined with plastic, green frogs graced the water lilies, and dragonflies took up perches on a giant bulrush!

I hope this book will inspire you and provide direction as you set off toward perhaps the most important outcome of the gardening experience—the creation of an enjoyable, living space that reduces the human impact on the environment and supports the needs of the wildlife with which we share our world.

I also hope your own experiences in creating a wildlife habitat will be as satisfying as mine. On behalf of the National Wildlife Federation, please accept our sincere appreciation for your part in restoring some of the natural diversity to America's backyards.

—Craig Tufts,
Chief Naturalist and Manager
Backyard Wildlife Habitat Programs,
The National Wildlife Federation

If you wish to receive recognition for your efforts to create a wildlife garden, please call 1-800-432-6564 to order the Backyard Wildlife Habitat Package (Item number 79921). The package includes reading on wildlife gardening, and a pre-paid application for NWF's Backyard Wildlife Habitat Program. Upon receipt of your completed application, NWF will send you a personalized certificate of achievement.

A Day in My Wildlife Garden

In 1989 my wife and I left the Catskill Mountains of upstate New York in search of warmer winters. I've been writing nature and gardening books since 1973, and I welcomed the opportunity for a change of scenery and climate. We settled in an old house in Asheville, North Carolina, and began to resurrect the garden—an acre of trees and thickets, abandoned beds and borders, and wildflowers, with a bit of lawn and a lovely 12-acre lake nearby.

Six years later, there's more than one battle without armament going on in our backyard, not 20 feet from where I sit in the comfort of my living room. It's early in December and a cold front has just passed through, dropping the temperature from a chilly but pleasant 40°F to a wet and unpleasant 20°F. Three gray squirrels have almost denuded a dogwood grove of their glowing red berries. They are now chattering away, the larger of the three attempting to dissuade the other two from interfering on his (or her) turf.

The squirrels dip and bounce on the dogwood branches, going from fairly thick wood to twigs that look as thin as a quill, but you know they'll never fall. The battle is, of course, an act. The claw feints are meant to scare, not draw blood. And as entertainment goes, it beats almost anything available at the mall, on TV, or at the movies.

And my squirrels have more of an audience than just me. At the corner of the garden where an ancient bank of rhododendrons begins to shroud the old stone wall, an eastern chipmunk sits watching the squirrels as intently as a wrestling fan watching a championship match on TV. His name is Somerset, and I know him by the notch in his left ear—a scar probably the result of fighting off the neighbor's cat.

Meanwhile, overhead in an old, tall oak, some crows are having it out with another squirrel who strives to defend his leafy penthouse bower from their talons and beaks.

Down at the corner of the lake where a narrow spit of land projects out into the water, our twenty-some resident ducks are engaging in verbal battle with three very large geese. Threats abound, but it's all talk. Nonetheless, it adds a streak of excitement.

Way above the tops of the oaks, three more crows are harassing a lone red-tailed hawk for reasons I'm not privy to. They all swoop, flutter, and then glide until they're finally out of sight.

This is what I can see. But underneath the carpet of leaves on the lawn and down in the earth beneath the grass roots or the perennials in the garden, where the icy cold of winter has yet to penetrate, wolf spiders dash about preparing nests. Various beetles blindly step over—and are occasionally nipped by—wandering ants. The butterflies of summer are long gone, but in the seeping warmth found at the edge of windows, small moths lie in wait for the few nights still ahead when temperatures will be warm enough for them to fly.

When the January thaw arrives (and winter has at least six weeks to go), that warm sun floating in a clear blue sky can lull you into a false sense of security. And it can lead to additional signs of life in the backyard: Mouse prints will become deceptively large as their molded edges pull away from the melt. (And the prints of a small dog will loom as large as those left by the hound of the Baskervilles.)

And I've yet to mention the wildlife that has gained access to our house: the insects that journey into the interior underneath the bark of the firewood; the common house mouse or the more original kangaroo mouse, who have a knack for finding holes and tunnels through house foundations that builders swear are perfectly solid; or the wandering centipede that winters in the far corners of the basement but occasionally loses its way.

This is what I see in one winter afternoon, though I live within the city limits, less than a mile from a gigantic mall and only about a half-mile (as the crow flies) from city hall.

When you start your own wildlife garden—as this book will help you do—you, too, will have many enjoyable and enlightening experiences observing the creatures that share our world.

Chapter One will get you started by introducing different types of wildlife habitats you may be able to create on your property. In Chapter Two, we'll give you all the basics for planting and caring for your garden. Chapters Three through Five will show you how to create the wonderful wildlife gardens we've previewed. Whether you fancy—and your property lends itself to—a shady woodland garden, a sun-drenched meadow or prairie garden, or a refreshing pond, pool, or streamside garden, you will find guidance here on each environment and the suitable plants to grow.

In Chapters Six through Eight, we'll talk about different kinds of wildlife and how to attract them to your backyard. Chapter Nine features profiles of backyard habitats certified by the National Wildlife Federation's Backyard Wildlife Habitat Program.

Remember that it's just as easy to create a wildlife garden as any other kind—and you'll find it's much more rewarding.

—Peter Loewer

OD in your own backyard

Chapter One

Creating a
Wildlife Habitat

Whether you simply add a brush pile and some shrubs,
trade some of your lawn for plants that will feed butterflies
and birds, or build a pond to attract aquatic creatures,
you can turn your garden into a place wildlife will call home.
This chapter shows you different kinds of wildlife
you can attract and the kinds of wildlife habitats
you can create. You will learn what wildlife needs to survive
and how to change your garden to meet these needs.
And you will find out how to choose a variety of plants
to attract wildlife to your yard.

Out in your own backyard

Even city dwellers can attract wildlife to a small garden. This tiny oasis near the entrance of a New York apartment building draws a variety of birds.

Your own yard is most likely teeming with wildlife. In most of North America, birds, mammals, amphibians, and insects abound. To create a habitat that will attract and nurture these wild creatures, the first thing you need to do is make your landscape more inviting to them by creating an environment that meets their needs. This will quickly bring everything from song birds and butterflies to toads and dragonflies, from squirrels and chipmunks to nocturnal creatures. After you become a patient observer, you will begin to see a world of living things just outside your door.

What lives in the backyard?

Most people live in and around cities and towns, but no matter where you live—in the suburbs or out in the country—each place attracts a different mix of wildlife. Manhattanites garden in the middle of a densely packed population center. But they can still watch house sparrows and house finches, nighthawks, pigeons, bluejays, cardinals, robins, and many migratory songbirds, especially on foggy days in spring or fall. City residents can also see a host of different insects, a surprising number of mammals and other animals, and many unusual plants that often grow in whatever pocket of soil their seeds may happen to find. They are also likely to observe ducks and geese flying north in spring and south in fall.

A wealth of wildlife thrives in the suburbs, where deer can be a threat to gardens and prized shrubs; where birds and frogs, then butterflies, herald the arrival of spring; and where garbage cans must be tightly sealed, not for protection from wandering dogs, but to foil the efforts of raccoons, opossums, crows, and other wild marauders.

Folks who live on farms or in rural areas also run into raccoons and 'possums and often see more deer and elk than they wish to count. Foxes—both red and gray—and coyotes are occasional visitors, and bears, moose, bobcats, and mountain lions have been known to wander past the front door on their way to a nearby snack.

By planting certain flowering annuals, perennials, and woody plants, you can attract butterflies—almost by species—to your garden, whether you live in town or in the country. You can also choose plants that will bring a wide range of birds. Hummingbirds flock to certain flowers, like bee balm (*Monarda* spp.) and cardinal flower (*Lobelia cardinalis*), or to hanging containers of sugar water, and will fly to the yard that offers these treats.

Add a protected birdbath, and birds will choose your yard for their summer vacations. To keep them around in winter, hang or install a bird feeder or two. Some birds like sunflower seeds, while others prefer niger seeds or millet.

Even late at night, there are visitors to the garden. The pollen of lily blossoms will attract moths and a number of fascinating insects. Small bats will eat insects on the wing, crickets sound their friendly chirps, and somewhere an owl will hoot.

Other forms of wildlife

Among the animals that live in landscapes devoted to wildlife are many insects. This remarkably diverse group of creatures contains more species than any other class of animals, ranging from hawk moths, which resemble hummingbirds, to regimented ant colonies and to those industrious scavengers, the earwigs.

One cardinal rule of nature states that everything depends on everything else. You can see this principle at work in your garden. When you begin to grow many flowering plants, insects will appear—and not only butterflies. Ants, beetles, bugs, bees, and wasps all love flower nectar. The insects will be followed by larger animals that dine on the insects. Insect larvae that live above and below the garden ground are, in turn, food for a host of mammals, including shrews, moles, and even voles.

Adding water to your garden will attract amphibians, including frogs and toads. Even tortoises and turtles can become part of your backyard world if you garden with their needs in mind.

Raccoons find their way into many gardens, although it is unusual to see them during the day. This inquisitive little fellow investigates a cosmos blossom.

What wildlife needs

Wildlife needs habitat diversity—that is, a variety of plants and a choice of housing sites. But within this diversity, you'll need to provide four features for wildlife to become year-round residents instead of occasional visitors: water, food, and cover—and, if all is well, a place to raise their young.

A source of fresh water is as important for wildlife as food and shelter. A birdbath placed on the ground serves as a drinking fountain for squirrels and other small mammals.

Water

It is easy for wildlife gardeners to focus on providing food and overlook an equally vital requirement of wildlife—water. Even a mud puddle will attract butterflies, and you'll draw butterflies and birds to a simple birdbath with a large perching stone in the center. If you'd like to attract mammals and amphibians, try a small pond made from a half barrel or a plastic watering trough. You might construct a pond with a fiberglass liner, a flexible pond liner such as polyvinyl chloride, or a heavy rubberliner; these can measure up to 26 by 46 feet with an 18-inch depth and are guaranteed for up to 30 years. If you have even more space, you can create a pond as large as half an acre or more, constructed by digging a hole or, with proper permits, damming a seasonal or permanent stream. (Note: Wildlife ponds work better when they are shallower and larger in area.)

The more varied an aquatic habitat you provide, the more wildlife you can attract. If a pond is large enough, migratory waterfowl such as ducks, geese, herons, and shorebirds may even stop by.

Food

Your habitat should offer plenty of food sources for animals. Natural sources are best—places where trees, shrubs, and plants supply the necessary seeds and fruits. You can also sprinkle bread crumbs or seeds directly on the ground or dispense them in various feeders that you can make in your basement workshop, order from a catalog, or buy at a local nursery or garden center. Even the more wary birds will come to feeders while you are close by as long as they have a sense of security while they eat. Every time you feed the birds, you may also be feeding the squirrels and their relatives, who seem to delight in showing people what they can do, especially to bird feeders. If you resent squirrels eating the bird seed, experiment with squirrel-proof feeders. But remember, squirrels eventually seem to find a way around most barriers. In the end, it's usually easier just to put out extra seed for the squirrels.

Site several feeding stations to afford visiting animals a sense of security while they remain visible to you, either from a well-concealed observation post or a window in your home. Try lighting food stations at night, perhaps with low-voltage lights, so you can watch nocturnal visitors, such as flying squirrels, feed. You can also use pizza trays or a garbage can lid to hold table scraps.

A place to stay

In addition to water and food, wildlife needs cover or places to hide. Cover offers wildlife protection from natural forces that may endanger them, such as weather and predators, as well as from you, their observer. Cover comes in many forms: Densely branched shrubs, evergreens both small and large, and meadow or prairie patches can all provide excellent protection. Cover also offers the perfect place for animals to raise their young. Specific plants can attract butterflies and moths, who stay to lay eggs after searching for nectar in the flowers. The same small pond or pool that will supply water for many animals will also meet the needs of toads, salamanders, and dragonflies because all of these animals need water for breeding purposes.

By carefully placing nesting boxes specifically suited for different bird species, as well as boxes specially designed for bats, you can attract a wealth of wildlife to your garden.

Finally, don't forget to include a spot where you can sit, watch, and enjoy the world of wildlife that you've brought to your own backyard. And if possible, plan your wildlife garden so as much of it as possiblE is visible from inside your house.

Many birds like to build nests in tree cavities. Here a young red-headed woodpecker peers out of its home in a dead tree.

Providing for wildlife

Zoning for wildlife gardens

Most local zoning regulations will not affect the design of your wildlife garden. Still, here are some basic guidelines to consider as you plan your wildlife habitat.

Start with your backyard. While you may eventually work in front as well, you can do as much as you want in back, free from the scrutiny of neighbors who might not understand your desire to bring wildlife into your yard. If you wish, you can make your front yard invisible by planting a mixed border of shrubs and perennials along the perimeter, but that can be an expensive proposition.

A fence can also hide your yard. But it's still best to consult with your local planning board, which will probably want to know how high your fence will be, before dragging out the posthole digger and visiting the lumberyard. All this makes the backyard the best place to begin your wildlife garden.

Most wildlife needs surprisingly little to thrive in your backyard. As we've said, wild creatures require water, food, and some shelter from the elements and their predators. And like you, they prefer what they perceive as a comfortable, friendly environment to a harsh and ugly one. Here are three ways to put out the welcome mat for wildlife in your backyard.

Take a low-maintenance approach

The less manicured you keep your garden, the more protection you provide for wildlife. The kind of wildlife garden that attracts the most living things offers a mix of plantings, and little of it should be perfectly groomed. Most wildlife has a built-in instinct for survival. Even predators, such as an all-powerful bear, a hawk, an owl, or a stinging insect, appreciate places to hide—if not from potential enemies, then from the weather or to protect their young.

If there is nothing in your backyard except a wide expanse of mowed lawn, little besides an occasional sharp-eyed, insect-eating bird will be attracted. So your first job is to provide hiding places.

Mix plant sizes

A mix of plants of different sizes will satisfy the varied security needs of a diverse array of animals. Larger animals prefer open woods or thickets where they can move through the branches with ease. Smaller creatures look for tangled areas of leaves and twigs that offer them plenty of protection, again without hampering their movements. Creating island beds with taller plants in the middle and progressively smaller ones toward the edges not only is an attractive design approach, but also provides valuable protection for a host of different animals. And placing larger plants to the back or on the outer edge of the garden with smaller plants in front is another good design technique. It's also a good idea to try to copy what you observe in the wild or any natural spaces in your neighborhood.

Combining plants of different sizes provides shelter for a variety of creatures. In this small water garden, a birdhouse perched on a stump is surrounded by grassy plants and small shrubs.

✒ Provide the foods that wildlife likes and needs

Animals, like people, have favorite foods (as anyone who has grown corn in the neighborhood of a raccoon family knows). Squirrels like nuts and other seeds; many birds have their favorite seeds, berries, and, of course, insects. Butterflies, which feed by day, are attracted to the colors of bright flowers and to their sweet nectars, while moths, which are night feeders, are lured by white flowers and powerful fragrances. Other insects—there may be hundreds or thousands of kinds that visit a plant-rich suburban yard—feed on nectar, while still others chew leaves or drink plant juices. Each species also has a range of predators that consider it a meal. If you want to attract a certain mammal, bird, or butterfly, it's your job to provide the foods they love.

Put your yard on the map

What is your USDA plant hardiness zone?

The ability of a plant to survive in the coldest possible temperatures determines its hardiness. The USDA Agricultural Research Center publishes a Plant Hardiness Zone Map which divides the United States and Canada (including Hawaii and Alaska) into 11 climate zones according to average winter minimum temperatures. Zone 1 represents minimum temperatures of -50°F, and subtropical Zone 11 has winter temperatures above 40°F. You can locate your zone by referring to the map on page 188.

When you have some idea of your actual backyard environment, the next step is to create a map that shows the natural features and man-made structures in your yard. Once you have gathered all of that information, you'll have an idea of how to proceed and what kind of a habitat you want to create.

Mapping your backyard

Mapping your yard is easy. All you need to begin your map is a sheet of plain paper and a pencil; graph paper is handy but not necessary. And remember, you don't need to be a great artist—just be clear.

One easy way to get a map of your property is to copy your property survey if you have one. If you don't, your municipality probably does, or you can hire a surveyor to create one.

If you're not working from a survey, start by measuring off your property outlines in feet, using a tape measure, and drawing the outlines on your paper. Don't forget to include some of your neighbors' property in the sketch; there might be something next door that you want to conceal, or an attractive feature directly adjacent that you wish to "borrow" or focus on for your property. If there is a group of trees on the property line, this might be a great opportunity to expand them. Your neighbors may even want to do the same on their property!

Put in all existing buildings, driveways, adjacent streets, waterways, trees, possible windbreaks, and obstructions such as existing fences or ditches you cannot fill. Be especially aware of those that will affect the amount of sunlight available throughout the year. Chart the direction of the prevailing winds with the help of your local weather service, and, using a compass, add the compass points for correct orientation. Add walkways, fences, objects such as mailboxes, and other relevant data, such as slopes, areas of shade, and attractive and ugly views.

Mark the locations of all your permanent plants and gardens, including your vegetable garden. If water spigots or sprinkler systems are in place, include them, too. And if you have young children at home, be

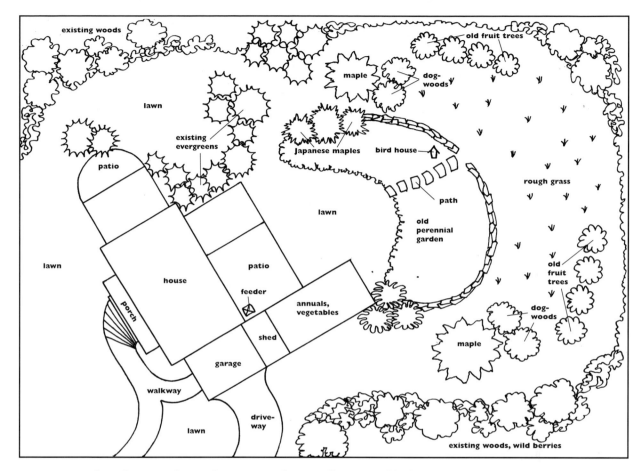

existing woods

lawn

existing evergreens

patio

lawn

house

porch

walkway

lawn

garage

drive-way

shed

feeder

patio

annuals, vegetables

Japanese maples

maple

dog-woods

bird house

path

old perennial garden

maple

dog-woods

old fruit trees

old fruit trees

rough grass

existing woods, wild berries

sure to note their favorite places of activity, such as sandboxes, and hiding places, as well as favorite shortcuts through the yard.

Note areas that have natural and artificial windbreaks, such as hedges, fences, and walkways, especially if you live in the colder areas of the continent. For example, your entire yard may be in Zone 5, where temperatures can fall to −20°F, but in a protected spot behind the garage, temperatures could be ten degrees warmer, making it a great place for less hardy plants or birds to wait out a winter storm.

Take a few Polaroid pictures of different areas of your yard, or take some 35mm pictures and have enlarged prints made. Later you can try out a few garden ideas by drawing on the prints with a felt-tip pen, just to give you a sense of how a particular idea might look.

When making a map of your yard or property, be sure to include existing features such as trees, driveways, sidewalks, fences or walls, the house, patios, and gardens.

Choosing a habitat

Once you have your map and can see exactly what's on your property at a glance, it's time to start thinking about what kind of wildlife garden you want. Three of the most popular are woodland, meadow, and water gardens. These gardens are discussed in detail in Chapters 3 through 5, but here's a brief overview of each to get you started. Consider wildlife as well as plants as you plan your garden—each type will attract different species.

Woodland gardens and thickets

Woodland gardens are ideal habitats for two reasons: Almost everyone has happy memories of hiking through the woods, and the protection provided by a woodland garden will attract many forms of wildlife. Most of us aren't lucky enough to live on large plots of land covered by stands of mature oaks and their acorns, but almost all of us have a few shade trees. You can turn a few trees into a woodland by imitating

In spring, a northeastern woodland garden glows with the warm colors of azaleas in bloom. Understory shrubs like azaleas are an important part of a woodland garden.

nature and underplanting them with smaller (understory) trees. There are many small trees that are large enough to give protection to wildlife, and some that provide flowers and fruits as food for them. In addition to a number of small evergreens, there are several small maples (*Acer* spp.), birches (*Betula* spp.), serviceberries (*Amelanchier* spp.), dogwoods (*Cornus* spp.), redbuds (*Cercis* spp.), and many more. By planting trees close enough together so that their mature canopies slightly overlap, you will leave room enough for healthy growth, plus ample protection for all the animals.

Thickets provide cover for many birds and mammals. You can plant them under trees or in the open. You can create thickets by planting various shrubs and bushes—and even vines—so close to each other that they become a tangled net of twigs and branches. For a quick thicket you might consider using plastic hoops (about five feet tall) and planting them with Virginia creeper (*Parthenocissus quinquefolia*), wild grapes (*Vitis* spp.), or trumpet honeysuckle (*Lonicera sempervirens*). A host of songbirds and other winter wildlife will cheerfully peck away at the fruit and seeds these plants provide, knowing that the interlaced vines will also offer them some protection from larger predators.

Meadow and prairie gardens

Although many gardeners think of meadow and prairie gardens as great sheets of wildflowers, the most successful ones mix wildflowers with grasses. Tallgrasses provide great protective cover for foxes, rabbits, shrews, and voles. When the grasses bloom and set seed, they provide food for many species of birds as well. Taller wildflowers, including the field asters (*Aster* spp.), milkweeds (*Asclepias* spp.), goldenrods (*Solidago* spp.), purple coneflowers (*Echinacea purpurea*), black-eyed Susans or orange coneflowers (*Rudbeckia* spp.), and many, many more, also flourish in the prairie or meadow environment. When these flowers bloom, they attract a host of butterflies by day—and often a surprising number of moths by night.

A sunny meadow flourishes in the open next to a wooded area. Meadow wildflowers attract butter-flies and bees, and the seedheads produced by the flowers and grasses provide food for birds.

Fish play in this small pond, sur-rounded by a wildflower meadow in the **NWF**'s model backyard wildlife garden in Vienna, Virginia. The pond also hosts frogs, dragon-flies, and other creatures. Pickerel weed blooms in the foreground.

Water gardens

Water is a lure to all wildlife, but a water garden also attracts its own special inhabitants. A small pond will soon attract frogs and salamanders, which in time will lay eggs. It will also bring water beetles, water bugs, dragonfly larvae, and even snails and small fish that may arrive as eggs on the feet of various water birds. Then in high summer, the true acrobats of the air appear: the dragonflies and damselflies—insects that not only enjoy the gift of flight but seem to enjoy life as well.

Other ways to attract wildlife

Some wildlife "gardens" are extremely easy to create. You would be amazed by the variety of wildlife that can find a home in a dead tree or a rotting log. Woodpeckers, flickers, and other birds will nest in dead trees, while still others will gather the mosses and lichens on the bark to use for lining their nests. Chipmunks will search along a fallen tree for insects to eat, and nuthatches will wander up and down a tree trunk in the same pursuit. Delicate ferns, colorful mushrooms, and other small plants will decorate an old rotting log or stump, turning an eyesore into an ornament.

Creating a brush pile in an out-of-the-way corner of your property is an extremely quick way to attract wildlife. Instead of hauling off tree trimmings, old Christmas trees, or leaves that haven't made it to the compost heap, make loose piles of this wonderful vegetative resource in a discrete part of your wild garden. Soon all kinds of animals will be using these piles for protection, searching for food, and perhaps even nesting in the comparative safety of their enclosures.

You may think a brush pile just looks messy, and indeed, in the middle of a manicured lawn it probably would. But if you have enough space that you can put a brush pile out of sight, it can be a valuable resource. You might be able to hide a brush pile behind a garage or shed, or perhaps grow Virginia creeper or other vines to cover the pile and make it less noticeable.

Rock gardens

Rock piles, rock walls, and rock outcrops provide both homes and hunting grounds for many animals. From chipmunks in the North to lizards such as skinks and racerunners in the central and southern states, creatures delight us as they search for the insects that dash about a rock garden or doze in the sun on a warm rock. Such gardens are also home to many harmless garden snakes, a large variety of beetles, and a host of spider species that nest in the hollows between the rocks. Chipmunks live between the rocks, too, and they love to sun themselves on top. To make a rock garden that appeals to this wildlife, honeycomb the rock pile or wall to create small cavities where creatures can hide.

The garden edge

Protected plants

Thousands of plants are considered endangered or at risk in the United States. So if you have any on your property, you have to be sure not to destroy them when you redesign. Both federal and state governments maintain lists of endangered plants. For information or a copy of the federal list, contact your county Cooperative Extension agent or the U.S. Fish and Wildlife Service. To get the list for your state or information on obtaining a copy, check your phone book for the office of the state Department of Agriculture or your state legislator's office.

Many private organizations are involved with the conservation of native plants, including the Nature Conservancy, the American Horticultural Society, the New England Wild Flower Society, the Missouri Botanical Garden's Center for Plant Conservation, the National Wildflower Research Center, and the World Wildlife Fund.

Of all the different backyard habitats you can create, nothing seems to be more popular with wildlife than the "edge" created where one type of habitat meets another. Such spots seem to draw birds, insects, and other animals like nothing else in the garden. Animals that are attracted to each habitat will mingle at the edge, while birds that would otherwise be hidden in one environment will openly move into another.

The edge habitat we see most often is where woods border a meadow, with low shrubs growing between the two as a transition. You can recreate this edge effect in your own yard where the lawn meets the flower beds, or anywhere else one landscape type abuts another.

You can even create more than one type of edge. For example, to create an edge community between a lawn and garden beds or borders, plant an area of low groundcovers in the front of the garden. Behind the groundcovers, and interspersed among them, add some low upright plants. Then, introduce plants in gradually increasing heights as you work your way toward the back of the garden. To create an edge between the garden and a nearby group of trees, put ornamental grasses and low shrubs in the back of the garden. Back the garden with tall shrubs, perhaps with vines growing through them, to provide a transition to the taller trees beyond.

Other edges include the area between the hedge or fence and the lawn, a vegetable garden and the yard, the deep water of a pond and its edge, a shallow pond and bog, a lawn and meadow, and the open space between the garden and a potting or tool shed in the rear. You can also create edges by planting "islands" or connected groups of trees, shrubs, and groundcovers. Wildlife can move safely through these plantings instead of being exposed while crossing an open lawn.

Aesthetically, edges are terrific. Instead of an abrupt ending to garden or lawn or shrubs and trees, one sweep seems to disappear into another. Not only will this be pleasing to your eyes, but your wildlife will also certainly approve.

Enjoying your habitat

Once you've created your habitat, take some time to sit back and enjoy it. You'll get the most out of your backyard wildlife garden if you keep good records. In the rush of planning a new garden, this task is often forgotten, but keeping track of which plants flourish and which ones fail—and recording your wildlife sightings—will make wildlife gardening easier and much more fun.

Keeping records with words and photos

Ideally, creating a wildlife garden will be a family activity, something to be remembered with warmth and affection during the years ahead. So keep copies of plant orders, and map changes as your landscape develops. Note the placement of feeders, bird houses and bat houses, and birdbaths, and keep a "visitors log." Take a few "before" and "after" photographs to document the changes and record wildlife visits. Then on a cold winter's evening, you can assemble all this material in an album of your achievements.

These low feeders filled with cracked corn and sunflower seeds are positioned at the edge of the lawn close to the cover of trees and shrubs. They attract mammals as well as birds like mourning doves.

Chapter Two

Getting the Garden Ready

Making your backyard a place that attracts wildlife
will take some time, but it is easier than you think—
and the wildlife is definitely worth waiting for.
This chapter will help you lay the groundwork and put out
the welcome mat for the birds and animals you wish
to entertain in your garden.

Fertile ground for wildlife

Soil is a complex mix of finely ground rocks and minerals, air spaces, water, and organic matter—both dead and decomposing—as well as living plants, animals, and microorganisms. The key to a healthy garden—and a garden full of living creatures—is healthy soil. If you are just starting to garden, it's important to know a few simple tricks for improving your soil.

In most new subdivisions, topsoil has been removed, leaving a subsoil that lacks many of the organic compounds and air spaces plants need to thrive. The repeated use of heavy equipment—or even walking over the same area day after day—compacts the soil, preventing easy entry of the water and air necessary to keep plants healthy. You can gradually solve the first problem by adding organic matter such as compost, which is easy to make from plant debris, fallen leaves, grass clippings, and other material, and you can alleviate the second by tilling and working in organic matter to break up compacted soil and allow air and water to nourish plant roots and beneficial soil microorganisms. Making raised beds and walking on paths (rather than all over your garden) are two other good ways to combat soil compaction.

Flowering dogwoods (*Cornus florida*) are part of springtime in the woodlands of the eastern United States, where they thrive in rich, humusy, slightly acid soil.

Continual applications of chemical fertilizers can also damage soil. Overfertilizing eventually kills many of the microorganisms soil needs to thrive. Earthworms are driven away by high fertilizer levels. And remember the importance of knowing your soil's pH so you won't try—and fail—to grow acid-loving plants in alkaline soil and vice versa. (See "About pH" on page 30.) If you suspect your soil may be overfertilized or that you may have a pH imbalance, you should take a soil sample to your local county Cooperative Extension Service office for testing. They will analyze your soil's pH and nutrient levels and recommend ways for you to adjust your soil's pH and nutrient content. Or you may wish to have your soil tested by a private laboratory, or purchase a home test kit and do it yourself. Laboratory soil tests usually check pH levels, and this can be done with a home kit as well.

Soil types in natural landscapes

Different soils will naturally support different landscapes. Loose, well-drained soil will host a number of plants not found in areas of solid clay or hardpan. In places where roadways have resulted in scooped-out banks on either side of the road, weeds that would refuse to grow a few feet away will readily take root. Soil and site conditions often determine the types of plants you'll find in a given place, since some like wet feet, others prefer dry, and their mineral and pH requirements vary.

Midwest prairie grasses and wildflowers While soils west of the Mississippi are often alkaline, those vast areas of the Midwest that were formerly prairie grasslands, covered by grasses and wildflowers, are usually neutral. Farther west, where drought is often the norm, soils are highly alkaline because rainfall is insufficient to flush salts from the soil. If your soil is too alkaline, you can lower pH by adding elemental sulfur. (See "About pH" on page 30.) But because recommendations will vary from place to place, we suggest you consult your local county Cooperative Extension agent for advice.

Indian grass (*Sorghastrum nutans*) is native to the prairies of the Midwest, where the soil is generally in the neutral pH range. Although long dry spells are common in summer, this region receives enough annual rainfall to keep salts from building up in the soil and creating alkaline pH levels, as happens farther west.

Eastern forest, woodland, and fields As a general rule, soil found east of the Mississippi tends to be acid. One exception is soil found in areas of limestone rock, which will be alkaline even when surrounded by acidic woodlands. The most commonly grown native plants will do quite well in the slightly acid soils of the East, but there are also plants that prefer more acid conditions.

About pH

Soil pH is its measure of acidity or alkalinity. If you read the pH scale starting at the left, you'll see that 3 or less represents very acid (or sour) conditions. The scale's center is neutral, represented by the number 7. The scale extends to the right past 11, with that end being alkaline (or sweet).

There are methods to correct most—but not all—pH problems. If your soil is too acid, for example, you can apply ground limestone at a rate of about 50 pounds to every 1,000 square feet of soil. If your soil is too alkaline, you can lower the pH by adding 10 pounds of powdered elemental sulfur per 1,000 square feet of soil. In the end, however, the most successful wild gardens use plants—native or introduced—that are matched to the conditions that nature provides. Reworking the natural pH in your backyard is possible, but not necessarily the best approach.

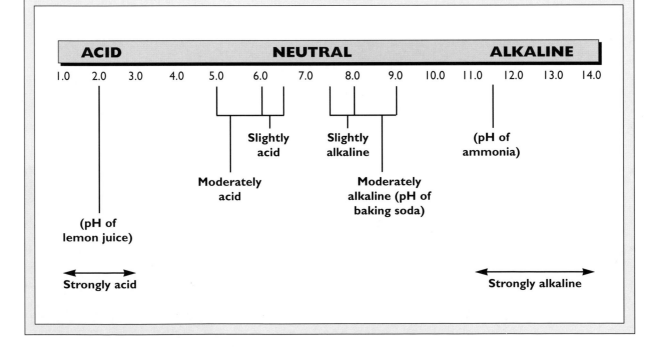

ACID						NEUTRAL					ALKALINE		
1.0	2.0	3.0	4.0	5.0	6.0	7.0	8.0	9.0	10.0	11.0	12.0	13.0	14.0

Slightly acid

Slightly alkaline

(pH of ammonia)

Moderately acid

Moderately alkaline (pH of baking soda)

(pH of lemon juice)

Strongly acid

Strongly alkaline

Planting trees and shrubs

Today most nursery-grown wildflowers are grown in their own containers, then moved easily from pot to garden. But shrubs, vines, and trees purchased from various nursery sources are sold either bare-root, balled-and-burlapped, or in containers.

With bare-root plants, open the package immediately to inspect the roots. If they're dark and dried up, return the plants and demand a healthy replacement or a refund. But if they're healthy and you can plant immediately, place the roots in a bucket of tepid water after carefully pruning away any that are broken or damaged. Dig a hole large enough to accommodate the roots comfortably, as deep and about twice as wide as the root ball. If the roots are spreading rather than taprooted, make a mound of soil in the bottom of the hole. Set the plant on the mound, and gently spread the roots over it and down the sides. A plant with a taproot or deep central roots can simply be set in the hole. Work soil around the roots carefully with your fingers. Fill the hole halfway with soil, then water well. Then fill the rest of the hole and water again. Finally, top-dress with compost.

When planting balled-and-burlapped plants in average soil, dig a hole 1½ to 2 feet wider and about as deep as the soil ball. In heavy soil, make the hole a few inches shallower than the root ball. Loosen the soil on the sides of the hole, but leave the bottom undisturbed. If your soil is sandy or heavy clay, you can give your young trees and shrubs a good start by digging the planting hole twice as wide as you would for average soil and amending the excavated soil by adding leaf mulch or composted leaves, up to a 1:1 mix. (Never use commercial peat because it is too acid and repels water.)

Place the plant in the hole. Fill the base of the hole with excavated soil or soil mix. Then loosen the burlap wrapping at the top of the ball and cut the ropes or remove the nails. If you know the burlap is natural, leave it to rot in place; otherwise, cut away as much as you can without disturbing the root ball. Fill in around the ball with soil, then water well. If needed, add more soil, then top-dress with compost.

With container-grown plants, remove the plant from the pot, and examine the root system carefully. If any roots wrap around the soil ball, tease some of the larger roots out of the ball with your fingers, or use a knife to make several vertical cuts up through the outside of the root ball. Set the plant in a hole wide enough to hold the root ball, with several inches to spare on either side. It should be deep enough so that the plant will be at the same depth it was growing in the container. Fill in around the roots with soil, then water thoroughly. Add more soil as needed to fill the hole, then top-dress with compost.

Creating a compost heap

Composting is one of the best things you can do for your garden. Adding compost will improve drainage, add nutrients, and bring both acid and alkaline soils closer to neutral. Compost makes a great mulch, too!

To begin composting, select a convenient spot in your garden where you can pile up vegetable matter collected from weeding, raking, and cutting grass, as well as kitchen scraps (vegetables, fruits, coffee grinds, tea leaves, and eggshells are all good).

In a bin, pen, or other structure, pile fresh vegetable matter that is succulent and high in nitrogen—or strawy horse or cow manure—in layers alternating with tougher, high-carbon materials like shredded leaves, newspaper strips, or even sawdust. A small amount of finished compost or good garden soil may be added from time to time to replenish the bacterial cultures that do the work of composting. Don't make the pile too big—3 feet wide and high is about right. When your heap gets this big, you should start a new one.

Once a week or so, you may wish to turn (or at least disturb) the pile to keep the ingredients mixed and aerated and the decomposition proceeding at an even pace. Your only other responsibility is to add moisture occasionally—especially in areas with little rainfall. A dry compost heap will not work.

The only items not suitable for composting are feces (not even a cat's); bones; meat scraps; fats or oils; plant material laden with herbicide, pesticide, or insecticide residue; diseased plants; and toxic materials such as sawdust from pressure-treated lumber. Also keep weeds that have gone to seed out of the compost pile—unless you want to spread the weed seeds through the garden with the compost.

Mix fresh grass clippings with dry materials such as shredded leaves; otherwise, they tend to mat down and produce an extremely unpleasant smell. Cut up larger items, such as whole melons or squash, before you add them to the pile.

Don't pack plants too close together in your garden. Since the hosta and irises growing near the fence will spread a bit from year to year as they mature, this gardener has allowed them room to spread out.

Don't overprotect or overplant

By overprotecting we mean making the soil too rich by using too much compost or fertilizer, so a plant that naturally can withstand hard knocks will grow accustomed to the good life, then keel over without a fight under adverse conditions. Once the plant has settled in, fertilize very sparingly—and never during its first year in the garden. Any native plant that is sited and planted well, then watched over for its first year, should never need a stronger fertilizer than compost.

Overplanting is putting too many plants too close together and not leaving enough room for them to grow properly. If bare earth bothers you, plant some annuals or groundcovers, or cover the ground with a layer of mulch until plants grow enough to fill in the gaps.

Chapter Three

Woodland Gardens

When you think of visiting woods or a forest, you'll know why woodland gardens are so popular. They bring to mind images of peace and restfulness, but also a sense of adventure: You never know what might be around the next bend of the path. When you create a woodland garden, you invite visitors to participate in a treasure hunt, where wildlife and beautiful woodland wildflowers are the hidden treasures.

Woodland wildlife

Two young raccoons are captured by the camera at night, peeking out from the foliage of a maple tree. Raccoons are particularly common in woodland gardens and are usually active after nightfall.

At any time of the year in any part of the country, you can find mammals, birds, reptiles, and other types of wildlife in the woods. After the comparative quiet of a typical winter, spring seems to be the busiest time in the woods, especially because most birds, mammals, and amphibians begin to breed and raise families. But except for sultry summer afternoons when even the wild creatures slow their pace, the hectic activity of everyday living continues well into fall and the first northern snowfalls.

Who'll come to your woods?

In addition to the ubiquitous squirrels (both red and gray) and the wandering raccoons, woodland gardeners may see deer, foxes, skunks, chipmunks, cottontail rabbits, opossums, and woodchucks on their property. Smaller wildlife, such as deer mice, voles, shrews, and moles, all enjoy the protection of the woodland garden.

If you garden in the country, you might sometimes even spot a bobcat or weasel running across the wooded path. Insects flit about, seeking food or mates, and birds fly in search of the insects. When the moon begins to rise, bats will ply the evening air looking for moths and other flying insects, and in some places nectar and fruit. You might even see a flying squirrel.

Many birds welcome the protection of the woods. While honeybees and most grasshoppers and butterflies prefer the open field or garden, dozens of beetles, bumblebees, moths, and even a butterfly or two—such as the great spangled fritillary and the mourning cloak—prefer the light shade of an open woodland lot.

Making tracks

Once you've learned to identify animal and bird tracks that are left in the mud—or on even a light brushing of snow—you'll become aware of just how much activity goes on right in your own backyard. It's amazing to see the number of tracks left in a single night while you're asleep or during the day while you're at work. Sometimes the tracks tell a dramatic story—like field mouse tracks that end abruptly where an owl swept out of the night.

In winter, mice often tunnel beneath the snow to escape predators, and their tracks may suddenly appear at the point at which they surfaced. Look for squirrel tracks between and around trees. The tracks of a flying squirrel may start in the middle of nowhere—on the spot where the airborne creature landed. The flaps of skin that form its "wings" leave a mark on either side of its footprints.

You will see gray squirrels in a woodland garden year-round. They are even active in winter, so provide food in every season.

Providing for wildlife

Wildlife, while not exactly fickle, will quickly move to the garden that provides what animals consider the best in water, food, and shelter. Once you provide wildlife with their needs, the invitation is out, and birds, mammals, and other creatures will respond enthusiastically.

Providing water

Water is one of the key elements of a woodland garden. Like people, birds and other animals need water to drink and to bathe in. Whether in the form of birdbaths, a small ornamental pond, or even half an old whiskey barrel, water is necessary if you hope to attract wildlife to your woodland garden.

And it's necessary all year—especially in winter when fresh water may be hard to find. Use a stock tank de-icer or electric heater to keep the water from freezing in winter. They're available from garden centers, bird supply stores and catalogs, water garden nurseries, and farm supply stores.

Keeping the feeders full

Even in a mature woodland garden, there will always be birds willing to empty your feeders for you. In virtually the entire United States, natural food supplies sustain populations of resident birds and other wildlife. But there may come a time when all the seeds and berries in the garden have been eaten, especially in areas that have hard winters. Then it is time for supplemental feeding, whether it's putting out corn for the squirrels or seeds for the birds.

It's a good idea to check the feeders before going away for a weekend to make sure they're full. If you're going to be away for an extended period of time, ask your neighbors to feed the birds and put out table scraps for the other animals. While it's not a matter of life or death, once you've started feeding your resident wildlife, they'll come to depend on you.

Belling the cat and leashing the dog

Cats chase birds, and dogs chase foxes and rabbits. Most communities have ordinances restricting free-ranging pets—though they rarely apply to cats—so remember to keep your dog on a leash or in the house when you're not around, especially in the early morning and around twilight, when many wild animals come out to feed.

Cats are more of a problem. If you can't keep a cat indoors all day, you should at least keep it in at night. And if that's impossible, be sure to put a bell on your cat's collar. The bell will warn hungry birds that are often so involved in capturing a sunflower seed or a tasty worm that they never spy the cat. Authorities are divided on the value of the bell—but it certainly can't hurt and probably can help.

Respecting your guests' ways of life

Some hawks eat songbirds; foxes eat cottontail rabbits; owls eat mice; snakes eat frogs; and squirrels have been known occasionally to eat baby birds as well as birds' eggs. If you have prey, you'll have predators. It's a simple fact of wildlife.

You can, however, take steps to control predation and reduce the presence of raccoons, opossums, and skunks in your woodland garden. Keep a tight lid on trash cans to discourage scavenging, and provide plenty of dense cover in which vulnerable wildlife can hide.

Protecting your precious plants

Don't forget that hungry wildlife (especially deer and rodents) may eat your plants. If you are an avid gardener and have rare or valuable plants, you can take measures to protect them from the wildlife that traverse your property.

Wrap tree trunks with wire or perforated tape to keep rabbits, mice, or deer from peeling off the bark. Put smaller plants inside wire cages. Rock gardens or other specialty plantings can be guarded by covering them with plastic bird netting.

Birds that nest in your woodland garden, like the shy wood thrushes shown here, will raise their young in the cover provided by trees and shrubs. But the family cat can pose a great threat to baby birds too young to fly. Keep your cat indoors if at all possible.

Creating a forest niche

Shredded leaves

When you walk through a wooded area, there are always leaves at your feet. The top layer of dry leaves is the remains of last autumn's leaf fall. If you delve below that top layer, you'll find other layers with leaves beginning to break down and crumble. Eventually, all these dead leaves will decay and become part of the rich, black humus of the forest floor.

When you're looking for a natural material to break up and improve the soil in your garden, use leaves from your own trees or ask your neighbors for some. The only equipment you might need is an electric or gas-powered leaf shredder because shredding speeds up the break-down process. (You can also shred leaves by piling them up and running over them with a lawn mower.) Shred the leaves, pile them up to compost, or spread them around as mulch and let them decompose. Soon you'll have the best woodland soil around.

Starting a woodland garden is almost like building a house: You need a careful plan and a good foundation. Without the shelter and food that trees and other plants provide, few living things larger than insects would enter your backyard. So before we begin to think about potential inhabitants, the garden must be planned.

A woodland garden includes deciduous and evergreen trees and shrubs, as well as understory plants such as ferns and shade-loving wildflowers. When considering plants for a woodland garden or any other kind of wildlife garden, remember that native plants will look more natural in addition to their attracting wildlife to your yard. Indigenous wildlife will use them for both shelter and food. Consult your local county Cooperative Extension agent, conservation groups such as the National Wildlife Federation, your state native plant society, and nearby botanical gardens for information on plants that are native to your area. Tell them you're planning to establish a woodland garden and ask them for their recommendations.

Trees for your woodland

If your woodland garden begins with an established forest, a great deal of your work is already done. But if you are planning to start your garden from scratch, here are some things to keep in mind. Unless you can afford to buy large trees—and they are very expensive—begin your efforts with a few young trees.

Try planting trees such as maples (*Acer* spp.), oaks (*Quercus* spp.), or beeches (*Fagus* spp.), or other species found in your part of the country. Space them properly, perhaps along the edge of your property, or if you have the room, create a small wooded patch by putting a large species in the center, then surround it with trees of smaller stature.

If you live next to a wooded area that will remain untouched over the years—or if your neighbors have such an area—you might consider planting more trees to extend the grove into your property. Deciduous trees provide wildlife with protection from predators from spring through fall as well as food in the form of nuts, seeds, and fruit. Birds, squirrels, and small mammals all depend on trees.

You may live in an area of tract houses from which a developer has removed all the trees, or you may own property where only some routine trimming and the planting of a few shrubs will enable you to create a woodland garden. If your property is entirely without trees, plant some before you do anything else. Choose a few fast-growing trees and you will be amazed to see how big a properly planted tree will grow in just five years. But don't get too attached to these trees, for as your garden matures, they may have to be removed to make room for more desirable slower-growing trees.

Birches are fast-growing trees that can form the nucleus of a small woodland garden. The gray birch (*Betula populifolia*), with clear yellow fall color, can reach a height of 20 feet in five years and is at home in the northeast and north central states. The river birch (*B. nigra*) is a good choice for most of the country, including the Southwest. The borer-resistant river birch cultivar 'Heritage' has beautiful salmon-white peeling bark.

You do not need a whole forest to have a woodland garden. Two trees will make a mini-woodland on a tiny lot, and three trees planted in a triangle will provide several shady zones for understory plantings.

Also, choose some trees for seasonal interest. Flowering dogwoods (*Cornus florida*), crabapples (*Malus* spp.), and hawthorns (*Crataegus* spp.) offer spring flowers and, later, fruit for birds and animals. Include evergreens such as rhododendrons (*Rhododendron* spp.), hollies (*Ilex* spp.), or any of the conifers to provide both winter color and protection for wildlife. Junipers (*Juniperus* spp.), pines (*Pinus* spp.), hemlocks (*Tsuga* spp.), and other evergreens provide protection year-round for rabbits and smaller animals while they search for food. Birds nest in their branches. Other creatures raise their young in the protected spaces under low-hanging boughs. You'll often find the cocoons of moths and many other species of insects in trees.

Staking young trees

For a year or two, until their roots adapt, young trees will need guy wires for support, especially in areas with high winds. When staking young trees, leave enough play in the lines to allow some flexibility in the upper part of the trunk because movement of the trunk in the wind is necessary to build up the tree's strength. Slide a section of hose around each wire where it touches the tree to keep it from cutting the bark.

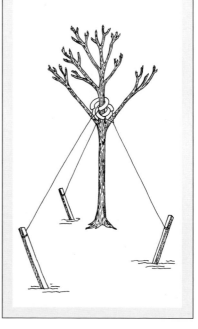

Shrubs for woodland gardens

Woodland shrubs and bushes include some fascinating and beautiful plants that thrive in the open shade of taller trees above. Especially noteworthy are three deciduous American natives: winterberry, viburnums, and blueberries. Winterberry (*Ilex verticillata*) is the only holly hardy in a northern winter, and it produces a wonderful show with loads of bright red berries in fall and winter. Plant winterberry at the edge of your woodland garden, and make sure you have both male and female plants for fruit set. Maple-leaved viburnum (*Viburnum acerifolium*) has late spring flowers that are followed in summer by blue-black fruits that birds and many mammals immediately eat. Many other viburnums make excellent woodland choices, too. Like us, birds also love the fruit of blueberries (*Vaccinium* spp.), and in autumn the plants' leaves turn a brilliant red, making them highly ornamental. Blueberry

The highbush blueberry (*Vaccinium corymbosum*) is an ideal plant for a woodland garden where the soil is moist, humusy, and acid. To be sure of getting blueberries that will be hardy in your garden, buy your plants from a local nursery.

Making a woodland path

A path is an important element of a woodland garden. It allows you and visitors to your garden to walk through the woods comfortably without muddy shoes or scratched arms and legs from low-hanging branches and thorny stems.

The best path is one that is made from natural materials, is unobtrusive, and twists and winds through the forest to provide new discoveries around every bend. Even in a small woods, a winding path will make the garden seem bigger.

Begin by clearing undergrowth, brush, and low branches from the path area. Remove branches and stems that hang over into the path. Open up planting areas alongside the path, too—this is an ideal place to plant some especially pretty wildflowers.

To make a natural-looking path, match the path materials to what's already on the ground. If the path runs under pine trees, mulch it with a layer of pine needles; under oak trees, mulch with fallen leaves.

If moss grows naturally in the area, you may be able to transplant enough of it to line the path. If you don't have enough moss to line the entire path, make your path of large stones sunk into the ground so their upper surface is even with the surrounding soil. Then plant moss between the stones.

To transplant moss, dig and rake the soil in the path area, then water until the soil surface is saturated. Allow the water to soak in. Dig up patches of moss elsewhere in the yard, taking some soil along with each patch. Press the moss patches onto the muddy soil in the path. Water again, this time with fish emulsion diluted to one-half the recommended strength.

If your garden is large enough to need a main path with one or more smaller paths branching off toward other parts of the garden, make the main path wider or of different materials than the side paths so visitors can find their way easily when walking through the woods.

hardiness varies widely—some species are better adapted to the South, some to the North—so buy locally for your woodland garden.

In addition to the larger shrubs are a number of shorter species called understory shrubs. Whether evergreen or deciduous, these shrubs provide summer cover and nesting sites for birds and small mammals; the fruiting shrubs produce food as well. There are hundreds of choices found across the United States. They include a favorite plant in the Northeast, the one-foot-high box huckleberry (*Gaylussacia brachycera*); the sand cherry (*Prunus pumila*) of the Midwest; the American elder (*Sambucus canadensis*) of the Southeast; and the redberry (*Rhamnus crocea*) that grows best in the warmer parts of the Southwest.

Currants (*Ribes* spp.) are also ornamental and fruit-producing, but do not grow them if there are white pines nearby—currants carry a fungus, white pine blister rust, that attacks the inner bark of white pines. Currants are hardy in Zones 3–7. Although native to the West, the Oregon grape holly (*Mahonia aquifolium*) is at home in most of the country (except areas with very cold winters—it will grow in Zones 5–9). Its spiny evergreen foliage looks like a giant coarse fern. In summer, it bears showy clusters of powdery, blue berries. Butterfly bush (*Buddleia davidii*) is a full-sun plant that attracts many butterfly species. Spicebush (*Lindera benzoin*) has aromatic leaves that are a favorite larval food of the spicebush swallowtail. Female plants will produce red berries if there's a male nearby. Spicebush is hardy in Zones 5–9.

Wildflowers

When you enter the shady world of woodland wildflowers, the list of plants that will prosper is huge. Even when dealing with plants sold by nurseries, numbers are in the hundreds. Many wildflowers bloom in early spring before leaves appear on woodland trees, then the plants go dormant and disappear by midsummer when the woods are in shade. Other wildflowers that are found in sunny spots in nature will actually do well when moved to an area of light shade. The choices are almost

The wild or eastern columbine (*Aquilegia canadensis*) is among our most beautiful native wildlflowers. The dainty woodland flowers have pointed red spurs that reminded Linnaeus of the talons of a bird of prey and inspired him to name the plant *Aquilegia*, from the Latin word for eagle.

endless, and good ones include American columbine (*Aquilegia canadensis*), asters (*Aster* spp.), goat's beards (*Aruncus* spp.), great Solomon's seal (*Polygonatum commutatum*), small Solomon's seal (*Polygonatum multiflorum*), green-and-gold (*Chrysogonum virginianum*), violets (*Viola* spp.), white snakeroot (*Eupatorium rugosum*), and wild gingers (*Asarum* spp.). See "Woodland wildflowers" on page 48 for more information on these flowers.

Don't limit your wildflower choices to the more obvious flowers. Grasses and sedges are flowering plants, too. And many of their seeds are important sources of wildlife food. Bottlebrush grass (*Hystrix patula*) and northern sea oats (*Chasmanthium latifolium*) will both do well in a woodland setting. So will a number of sedges, attractive grasslike plants that are also producers of seed. The larvae of the beautiful satyr and wood nymph butterflies feed on grasses and sedges.

Ferns and mosses

Of all the plants at home in a woodland garden, perhaps the most beautiful of all are the ferns. From the frigid woods of the Far North to the Deep South, where the cold breath of winter rarely blows, there are countless ferns for the woodland garden. Although they have limited value for wildlife (deer will eat them when hungry), they impart

Buyer beware

Don't hesitate to ask questions when buying wildflowers as plants from nurseries. Most plant suppliers believe in conservation and never dig up wildflowers in woods and fields to sell to unsuspecting buyers, but a few do. In some places, wild plant populations are being decimated by unscrupulous collectors and dealers.

So always buy from dealers who are proud of propagating plants at their nurseries. Make sure they sell nursery-propagated plants; plants labeled "nursery-grown" may have been dug from the wild and potted up in the nursery.

such a natural look to the woodland scene that it's hard to imagine a wildlife garden without a few species.

Three of the best ferns for woodland gardens are lady fern (*Athyrium filix-femina*), shield ferns (*Dryopteris* spp.), and Christmas fern (*Polystichum acrostichoides*). Lady fern grows wild across much of North America. It has finely divided, lacy fronds and will spread rapidly, making it a good groundcover. It is hardy in Zones 3–8. Shield ferns (also called wood ferns) grow 1½ to 4 feet tall, depending on the species, with triangular fronds composed of small, flat leaflets. Most are hardy in Zones 3–8, but hardiness varies with the species. Christmas fern, hardy in Zones 3–9, grows 1 to 3 feet tall, with stiff, dark green fronds. The larger western sword fern (*P. munitum*) grows 3 to 5 feet high and is hardy in Zones 5–9. All these ferns need moist but well-drained, humusy soil with an acid pH, and shady conditions.

The mosses are lowly plants that are spread by windblown spores and can be found growing in the cracks of city sidewalks, in the poorly drained soil around suburban malls, and throughout the woods and fields of temperate America. They, too, are of limited food value in the wildlife garden, but small birds like hummingbirds often line their nests with mosses. And there's nothing like moss for adding that cool forest feeling to a woodland garden. See "Making a woodland path" on page 43 for information on transplanting moss to a woodland garden.

No woodland garden would be complete without ferns. Their lush foliage is ideal for edging a shady path or providing cover for a low birdbath or feeder, as in this garden.

Woodland trees and shrubs

American holly (*Ilex opaca*), usually 20 to 30 feet but sometimes 40 or 50 feet tall. Pyramidal to irregular in shape. Toothed leaves of dull green in the species, but many cultivars are available with glossy, dark green foliage (and are less troubled by pests and diseases). Female trees produce red berrylike fruits in fall; plant both males and females to get fruit. American holly needs fertile, moist but well-drained soil with an acid pH; it tolerates cold temperatures but not drying winter winds. Hardy in Zones 5–9.

Arrowwood viburnum (*Viburnum acerifolium*), to 6 feet tall. Dark green, maple-like leaves turning shades of reddish purple in fall; blue-black fruits mature in fall. Grows well in dry shade, tolerating heavier shade than many shrubs. Hardy in Zones 3–8.

Crabapples (*Malus* spp.), many species and cultivars available, most growing from 15 to 25 feet tall. White, pink, or red flowers bloom in spring, followed by small red or yellow fruits in summer or fall. Crabapples prefer moist but well-drained soil with an acid pH. They like sun; plant along the edges of a woodland. Most are hardy in Zones 4–8, depending on the species or cultivar.

Gray birch (*Betula populifolia*), 20 to 40 feet tall. Usually multistemmed, with slender branches, often with drooping tips; glossy green leaves turn yellow in fall. Tolerates a wide range of soils, except for very alkaline ones. Hardy in Zones 3–7.

Hawthorns (*Crataegus* spp.), 15 to 30 feet tall, depending on the species. Broad, spreading form and thorny branches. Small white flowers in spring are followed by red fruits in fall. A thornless variety of cockspur hawthorn (*C. crus-galli* var. *inermis*) is available. Hardy in Zones 3–7, depending on species.

Heritage river birch (*Betula nigra* 'Heritage'), 40 to 70 feet tall, is pyramidal to rounded in shape. The attractive, peeling bark is salmon-white on young branches, darkening to orange-brown with age. River birch likes moist, acid soil but tolerates drier soils, too. This cultivar is especially resistant to borers. Hardy in Zones 4–9.

Oregon grape holly (*Mahonia aquifolium*), 6 or sometimes 9 feet tall. Evergreen shrub with glossy, leathery, dark green compound leaves consisting of pairs of spined leaflets along a central stem, similar to ferns; powdery blue-black fruits resembling grapes appear in late summer or early fall and may persist into winter. Needs moist but well-drained soil with an acid pH. Hardy in Zones 5–8.

Spicebush (*Lindera benzoin*), to 12 feet tall, with a loose, rounded form. The light green aromatic oval leaves turn bright golden yellow in autumn. Bright red fruits produced in fall. Slow to become established, it grows best in moist but well-drained soil, but will also tolerate drier conditions. Hardy in Zones 4–9.

Winterberry (*Ilex verticillata*), 10 feet tall and wide, is a dense shrub. Oval leaves have a good green color; bright red berries in fall persist well into winter if birds don't eat them all. Does best in moist, humusy soil with an acid pH. Hardy in Zones 3–9.

Woodland wildflowers

American columbine (*Aquilegia candensis*), to 2 feet tall. Delicate plant with compound, lobed leaves; yellow flowers with red spurs bloom in spring and early summer. Native to the eastern U.S. Zones 3–8.

Goat's beard (*Aruncus dioicus*), 5 to 7 feet tall. Ferny, compound leaves; airy spires of tiny white flowers in summer. Zones 3–7.

Great Solomon's seal (*Polygonatum commutatum*), to 8 feet tall. Arching stems with two rows of pointed, oval leaves 6 inches long; slender tubular white flowers dangle from the stems in May, followed by dark berries later on. Small Solomon's seal (*P. biflorum*) grows to 3 feet tall and is a more attractive garden plant. Both species are U.S. natives. Zones 3–7.

Green-and-gold, goldenstar (*Chrysogonum virginianum*), to 1 foot tall. Deep green, oval leaves with toothed edges; starry yellow flowers about 1½ inches across from April to June. Zones 6–9.

Showy aster (*Aster conspicuous*) to 2 feet tall. A western species, oval to oblong leaves; violet flowers. Zones 4–8.

Violets (*Viola* spp.). Under 1 foot tall. Heart-shaped, narrow, or compound leaves; small flowers on slender stems are violet, blue, white, or yellow, depending on species. Most are hardy to Zone 4 or 5, and also grow quite far south. Check local nurseries for species suited to your area.

White snakeroot (*Eupatorium rugosum*), to 4 feet tall. Heart-shaped leaves; clusters of tiny white flowers in late summer and early fall. Zones 3–7.

Wild gingers (*Asarum* spp.), to 7 inches tall, depending on species. Glossy, deep green, heart-shaped to rounded leaves; inconspicuous brownish flowers in spring. Roots smell like ginger. Useful as groundcover. Zones 3–9, depending on species.

Caring for woodland plants

Take advantage of periodic walks through your woodland garden to check on the health of your plants and spot problems before they become insoluble. Plants growing in conditions to their liking are vigorous and healthy, so they're able to survive pests and diseases that would destroy weaker plants. But problems can still occur. Remove bagworms and tent caterpillars before the pests cause serious loss of foliage. Prune diseased branches affected by canker or fire blight, dipping your shears in rubbing alcohol or bleach solution after each cut. Remove diseased plant material from the garden and dispose of it. Do not put it on the compost pile or chip or shred it to use as mulch.

Native plants in woodland gardens generally tolerate fluctuations in moisture and temperature brought on by weather conditions. But sometimes nature throws a curve, and a period of extended drought occurs. Once the plants are established, they can generally withstand a great deal of abuse if they are adapted to your area—especially if they're mulched with a thick layer of compost or shredded leaves. However, if you see signs of wilting in the woodland garden, give nature a hand by providing some water. Newly planted ferns, wildflowers, trees, and shrubs in their first year of residence in the garden are most vulnerable.

There are some seasonal maintenance chores as well. Perennial wildflowers may eventually become crowded after several years in the garden and will bloom less. You can divide and replant the clumps of roots to rejuvenate the plants. In the fall, divide and transplant perennials that usually bloom in spring and early summer; in the spring, divide late bloomers. Be sure to do any planting or transplanting at least a month before you expect your first serious frost to give plants time to establish roots before the ground freezes.

You may even find it necessary to take measures to control weeds. Nature abhors a vacuum, and bare earth won't stay bare for long. Unless plants are set so close together that they cover the soil com-

The value of dead trees, stumps, and logs

Don't forget that a dead tree, hollow log, or stump can be almost as valuable in the woodland garden as a living tree. Strange and beautiful fungi often grow on the dead bark, and so do mosses and lichens. Birds like woodpeckers and nuthatches, looking for nesting insects, attack the wood, and many birds and small animals use dead trees for nesting. Fallen logs can make beautiful, natural-looking benches for the woodland garden. Stumps also make great plant containers. You can hollow them out at the center, then fill them with soil and plant them with wildflowers, ferns, or ivy.

pletely, unwanted seedlings and weeds will find and move into any empty spaces. That's another reason why mulch is so important. Spreading a layer of shredded leaves, compost, or other organic mulch helps check the growth of weeds, conserves water, and keeps roots cool. Your garden will look far more attractive if it is neatly mulched than if it's left to grow weedy. And it will be far less work.

Where wildlife is concerned, sometimes the best plant care is benign neglect. Out in your woodland garden, the trees and other plants are alive and growing—but continually shedding, too. Rain falls, storm winds blow, and branches and twigs drop to the ground to be joined by fallen leaves, bits of paper blown from other yards, spent blossoms, and eventually seedpods and a rush of autumn leaves. If you must assist nature by cleaning up, pick up twigs, branches, and fallen leaves, then shred them and return them to the garden as mulch. If you can tolerate a buildup of twigs and leaves in part of your landscape, you'll attract more wildlife. Birds and small mammals will respond to the increased food and shelter these brushy areas provide.

Pruning dead and damaged wood

In a woodland garden, you will rarely need to prune trees and shrubs to improve their shape or limit their size. Pruning will be pretty much limited to removing dead and damaged wood, or perhaps to removing lower branches of older trees to let in more light for smaller plants. When working with trees and shrubs in the woodland garden, remember the following:

- Remove branches and twigs that rub against each other.
- When pruning trees, never cut a branch flush to the trunk. Cut right next to the collar (a ridge of thickened tissue where the branch meets the trunk) when removing a branch. This allows a callus to form quickly and protects the interior wood of the trunk from disease. Cutting into the collar or leaving a branch stub beyond the collar increases the chances of disease attacking the exposed wood.

In a woodland garden, you should allow trees to assume their natural form. The only pruning needed is to remove dead or damaged branches when necessary and to eliminate crossed branches that rub together and could result in bark damage.

- Always use a sharp, clean knife, saw, or pruning shears. If you are removing diseased wood, cut back to healthy tissue, and sterilize your tools after each cut by dipping in rubbing (isopropyl) alcohol or a solution of one part liquid chlorine bleach to nine parts water.

- Never cover wounds with pitch, paint, or wound dressings. Sealing the wound from the open air invites infection by fungi and bacteria.

- To remove a large or heavy branch, make your first cut from below the branch, about 1 foot out from the trunk; cut only one-third of the way through the branch (this prevents the bark of the trunk from tearing when the branch is removed). Make the second cut from above, about 2 inches out from the first cut; cut all the way through the branch. Your final cut removes the short piece that's left but also leaves the branch collar.

- Finally, always be careful when using power equipment in the garden. If you're climbing a tree, make sure that another person is on the ground in case you need help. If the branch that needs pruning is high in the tree, don't take chances—call a professional arborist or tree pruning service.

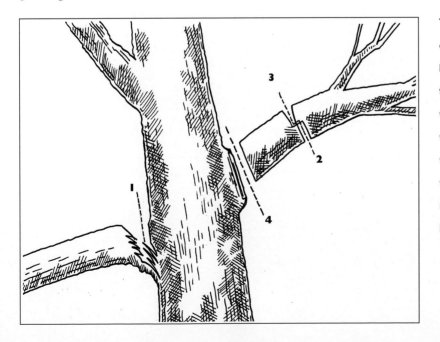

To remove a large branch without causing damage, as in the left branch pictured here (1), make the first cut a foot from the trunk, cutting up from the bottom (2). Make the second cut near the first, this time cutting down and completely through the branch (3). Then remove the stub flush with the branch collar (4).

Chapter Four

Meadow and Prairie Gardens

Two of the world's most beautiful sights are bright, sunny meadows and wide open prairies, both carpeted with a rich mixture of colorful wildflowers and tall grasses. The plants wave back and forth in the slightest breeze, while butterflies—rarely seen in wooded landscapes—flutter from blossom to blossom, all under a bright blue sky. These open grasslands are places of peace, and their "amber waves of grain" represent the spirit of the American environment.

The meadow environment

A wild meadow is a mixture of native grasses and wildflowers that grow in forest clearings, or in open fields where the soil is rocky or of poor quality. The meadow is a transition stage between the first tough colonizers, such as ragweed, and the trees that will later take hold and eventually return the area to woodland. Meadows are found in the eastern part of the United States, where there is more rainfall than in the prairies of the Great Plains.

A meadow garden is mostly green. It has tall, green grasses with dots of color provided by buttercups (*Ranunculus* spp.), oxeye daisies (*Chrysanthemum leucanthemum*), ironweeds (*Vernonia* spp.), cinquefoils (*Potentilla* spp.), milkweeds (*Asclepias* spp.), asters (*Aster* spp.), and thistles (*Cirsium* spp.), among other flowers. Butterflies fly from flower to flower, while birds hunt for bugs or seeds and hawks circle high above, swooping on the high air currents of summer.

Although Native Americans burned vegetation to create meadows for thousands of years in the East, most of today's meadows are fairly recent to the contemporary scene because they appeared after cleared woodland (which had become farmland) went back to nature as America changed its economic habits over the last century.

Gardeners can create meadow gardens on their own property, but there are certain ground rules that must be followed or success will be fleeting. If you follow the instructions in this chapter and are patient, the end result can turn a formerly boring and labor-intensive grass lawn into a home for birds, flowers, butterflies and other beneficial insects, plus a variety of small mammals.

Meadow wildlife

When you create a meadow garden, you may see familiar mammals like eastern cottontails, woodchucks (animals that are marvelous to watch but can often do mischief in the vegetable garden), meadow voles, meadow jumping mice, deer mice, and white-tailed deer that will gather to eat grasses or respond to a salt lick. Occasionally, other

If you are lucky, a fox may visit your meadow garden. Here, a red fox kit sits amid wildflowers and grasses in a Minnesota meadow.

animals will pay you a visit: shrews (which search for insects), red and gray foxes, skunks, and even weasels that hunt for mice and other small mammals in the grass cover.

Birds that live or forage in meadows include red-winged blackbirds, bobwhites, meadowlarks (which build their nests in the tallgrass), American goldfinches (who love thistle seed), barn swallows, kingbirds, song sparrows, and tree swallows. If you are lucky, eastern bluebirds may call your meadow home.

But the meadow garden is especially valuable for the marvelous range of insects it attracts. Bumblebees, hawk moths, and a wide variety of butterflies will be lured to meadow flowers. If your plants include some evening primroses (*Oenothera* spp.), you will also see a large selection of moths, beginning in early evening.

You will have to mow your meadow once each year—and two or three times during the first year—to give the wildflowers a chance to stand up against weedy plants. But it's well worth the effort. Late in the winter, before next year's growth begins, is the very best time to mow the meadow.

This fawn seems to be sniffing a daisy in a summer meadow. Deer frequently come to meadows to eat the succulent grasses; perhaps this youngster is trying to figure out if daisies belong on the menu.

Meadow plants

Consider all the plants that flourish along roadsides and other open sites and you'll realize that there is an incredible number of native American and naturalized wildflowers and grasses you can grow in a meadow garden. The basic problem is having too many to choose from, not too few. Grasses that do especially well in meadow gardens include wild ryes (*Elymus* spp.) and bottlebrush grass (*Hystrix patula*). The choice of wildflowers includes yarrows (*Achillea* spp.), pearly everlastings (*Anaphalis* spp.), false indigos (*Baptisia* spp.), Queen Anne's lace (*Daucus carota* var. *carota*), cardinal flower (*Lobelia cardinalis*), common pokeweed (*Phytolacca americana*), evening primroses (*Oenothera* spp.), obedient plant (*Physostegia virginiana*), and many more. You can also plant some shrubs in your meadow to produce flowers attractive to bees and butterflies, and berries for birds and mammals. Blueberries (*Vaccinium* spp.), sapphireberry (*Symplocos paniculata*), and American cranberry bush viburnum (*Viburnum trilobum*) are three good choices. See "Meadow plants" on the opposite page and "Wildflowers for meadows" on page 58 for descriptions.

This eastern meadow garden features several classic wildflowers, including golden yellow black-eyed Susans (*Rudbeckia hirta*) and pale pink New Jersey tea (*Ceanothus americanus*). For an extra shot of summer color, the gardener has also planted purple campanulas among the grasses.

Meadow plants

American cranberrybush viburnum (*Viburnum trilobum*), to 12 feet high and wide. Leaves have three pointed lobes, turn yellow to purplish red in fall; clusters of white flowers in spring; red fruits in fall that are edible if the birds leave any. Grows best in moist but well-drained, reasonably fertile soil. Thrives in full sun or partial shade. Zones 2–7.

Bottlebrush grass (*Hystrix patula*), 4–6 feet tall in flower. Olive-green foliage is 8–12 inches long; beautiful seedheads resemble bottlebrushes. Moist soil, some shade. Zones 5–9.

Canada wild rye (*Elymus candensis*), to 5 feet tall (below). Flat leaf blades; upper leaf surface is rough, sometimes hairy; dense, stiff, bristly seedheads. Zones 2–7.

Common pokeweed (*Phytolacca americana*), 4–8 feet tall. Attractive large green leaves; showy, flat clusters of small white flowers, dark purple berries favored by birds and raccoons. Zones 5–9.

Hardhack (*Spiraea tomentosa*), 3–4 feet tall. Bushy plants with attractive serrated oval leaves; pink spires like cotton candy. Zones 5–8.

Highbush blueberry (*Vaccinium corymbosum*), 6–8 feet tall. Glossy oval leaves turn red in fall; white or pinkish bell-shaped flowers in late spring and early summer; sweet, flavorful deep blue berries. Suited to damp spots. Zones 4–8.

Sapphireberry (*Symplocos paniculata*), spreading shrub or small tree to 20 feet tall. Elliptical leaves to 4 inches long; clusters of small, white flowers in late spring; turquoise berrylike fruits in fall. Zones 4–8.

Slender wild rye (*Elymus villosus*), 3–4 feet tall. Softly hairy on upper leaves; attractive foxtail-like seedheads. Zones 3–8.

Virginia rose (*Rosa virginiana*), 3–6 feet tall. A lovely small rose. Reddish canes with glossy green foliage; single, pink, 2-inch flowers in June. Good fall color and showy red fruits. Zones 3–8.

Canada wild rye

Wildflowers for meadows

Blazing-star (*Liatris* spp.), 1–5 feet tall. Grasslike leaves in thick whorls; dozens of showy, fuzzy spikes of white, pink, or magenta flowers in summer. Zones 2–9, depending on species.

Black-eyed Susan (*Rudbeckia hirta*), 1–3 feet tall. Coarse, oblong leaves; 2- to 3-inch yellow daisy-like flowers with purple-brown centers in summer. Drought-tolerant, long-blooming plant that thrives in hot weather. Plants are short-lived perennials grown as self-sowing annuals. Birds enjoy the seeds.

Blue false indigo (*Baptisia australis*), 2–5 feet tall. Attractive blue-green leaves; blue pea-like flowers in showy spikes in late spring and early summer, followed by gray-black seedpods called Indian rattles. Zones 3–9.

Cardinal flower (*Lobelia cardinalis*), 2–4 feet tall (below left). Upright plants with oblong to lance-shaped leaves; showy, 2-foot spikes of fire-red flowers in summer. Plant favors wet spots. Attractive to hummingbirds. Zones 2–9.

Common evening primrose (*Oenothera biennis*), 1–5 feet tall (below right). Biennial; large lance-shaped leaves, sweet-smelling, yellow, saucer-shaped flowers that bloom in the evening in late spring and summer. Zones 3–8.

Common milkweed (*Asclepias syriaca*), 3–5 feet tall (opposite, left). Upright, with large, fleshy, oval leaves; small clusters of dusty rose, lavender, or even purple flowers. Home to monarch butterflies and food for their caterpillars. Zones 4–9.

Common sneezeweed (*Helenium autumnale*), 3–5 feet tall. Bright green, toothed, lance-shaped leaves; clusters of fall-blooming, yellow to mahogany daisy-like flowers. Do well in damp soil. Zones 3–8.

Cardinal flower

Common evening primrose

Common yarrow (*Achillea millefolium*), 1–3 feet tall. Ferny green foliage; small, white, summer-blooming flowers in flat clusters. Zones 3–9.

Goldenrods (*Solidago* spp.), 1–5 feet tall. Dark green oval- to lance-shaped leaves; thick clusters of small bright yellow to golden flowers on tall spires in summer and fall. Zones 3–9, depending on species.

New England aster (*Aster novae-angliae*), 3–5 feet tall (below right). Small narrow leaves, small star-like daisy flowers in bright blue, rose, violet, or even magenta, depending on the cultivar, with yellow-orange centers. Blooms in late summer. Zones 3–8.

Obedient plant (*Physostegia virginiana*), 3–5 feet tall. Shiny green foliage; many pink, snapdragon-like flowers in thick spikes on square stems. Blooms in late summer. Zones 3–9.

Pearly everlasting (*Anaphalis margaritacea*), 1–3 feet tall. Narrow, whorled leaves; clusters of small, white, papery flowers in late summer. Zones 3–8.

Purple coneflower (*Echinacea purpurea*), 2–4 feet tall. Shrubby plants with oval leaves; large, long-lasting, daisy-like, downturned purple-pink flowers with orange-to-brown centers, in mid to late summer. A butterfly plant; birds eat the seeds. Zones 3–8.

Queen Anne's lace (*Daucus carota* var. *carota*), 2–4 feet tall. Biennial with ferny foliage; large, flat clusters of tiny white flowers borne in summer. This self-sowing beauty is perfect in the meadow garden, even though an alien plant. Zones 3–10.

Stiff coreopsis (*Coreopsis palmata*), 2–3 feet tall, bright yellow, daisy-like flowers in July. Zones 4–8.

Sundrops (*Oenothera fruticosa*), 1½–3 feet tall. Deep green lance-shaped leaves; day-blooming, 1½- to 2-inch shiny, yellow saucer-shaped flowers like evening primroses. Blooms in late spring and summer. Zones 4–8.

Common milkweed

New England aster

The prairie environment

When the colonial French arrived in America, they called the grasslands of the Midwest a *prairie*, meaning a European-style meadow. A 1767 survey map termed the upland beyond the city of St. Louis and north of the Missouri River a "huge prairie that will hold many settlers." When Lewis and Clark left Missouri in 1804, they chose the term *great plains* for the vast seas of grass beginning to the west of Indiana and extending in various guises to California. But eventually, the word *prairie* came into common use.

Early pioneers found prairie grasses that grew as high as 12 feet and stretched to the horizon in an unbroken sea of green. It was not until the snows of winter broke the grass stems to the ground that the true lay of the land could be seen.

There are three distinct types of prairie, each defined by the height of its dominant grasses. First is the tallgrass prairie that once covered vast areas of the Midwest, including sections of Ohio, Indiana,

Big bluestem (*Andropogon gerardii*) and gray-headed coneflower (*Ratibida pinnata*) grow together in a tallgrass prairie in Iowa. Of the three types of prairies, tallgrass prairies have the richest soil and receive the most rainfall.

Missouri, Iowa, Kansas, Nebraska, South Dakota, and North Dakota, and extended up into Canada. The soil in tallgrass prairies is fertile and rainfall is usually plentiful. Grasses grow tall—5 feet or higher.

Then there's the mixed prairie that runs from North to South, through both of the Dakotas, most of Nebraska and Kansas, and central Oklahoma, and down into north central Texas. The region of mixed prairies has a number of different soil types, and average annual rainfall is less than in tallgrass prairies but greater than in shortgrass prairies. The grasses, too, are intermediate in height, averaging 2 to 4 feet tall.

Finally, there's the shortgrass prairie, which predominates in an area bounded on the west by the Rocky Mountains, to the east by the mixed prairie, and running from Montana through eastern Wyoming, eastern Colorado, western Kansas, the Oklahoma panhandle, the northern panhandle of Texas, and a slice of eastern New Mexico. The shortgrass prairie is the driest of the three types, and its dominant grasses are the shortest, usually under 2 feet high. Plants must be drought-tolerant to survive in the shortgrass prairie.

In all these prairie types, the plant life consists of dominant grasses growing in unison with hundreds of different kinds of wildflowers, along with some shrubs, bushes, and trees. All prairies grow on soil that varies in pH from alkaline to slightly acid, much of it sitting on a stable bedrock covered by sandstones, limestones, and various shales.

When we think of prairies, we usually picture flat plains extending as far as the eye can see. But for the backyard gardener, one of the best ways to use a prairie is on a slope. If your property slopes down to the street, it can be both difficult and dangerous to mow. But if you replace the lawn with colorful prairie grasses and wildflowers, you'll cut down on maintenance, add an eye-catching landscape feature, and create privacy (since many prairie plants are fairly tall). Here's a tip, though: Put up an "American Prairie Garden" sign in front of your new landscape, explaining the plants and wildlife in your prairie. Your neighbors will be more tolerant of your new garden if they know what's going on.

Prairie wildlife

The greater prairie chicken looks a bit like a barnyard fowl but makes its home in the tallgrass prairie.

The horned lark, found in prairies, open fields, and occasionally golf courses, is noted for its trilling song.

Cars speed along the interstates of the Midwest, but few of the drivers realize the number and variety of mammals, birds, insects, and other creatures that live in the protection of the prairie plants along the roadsides. Some, like the American robin, the red-winged blackbird, the American goldfinch, and even the deer mouse, live throughout North America. Easterners may already be familiar with the turkey vulture (often improperly called a buzzard), red-tailed hawk, mourning dove, cliff swallow, and northern harrier. These birds may be found living through much of the eastern landscape as well as the prairie. But as you travel west from the Atlantic, new species join the flocks. There are dozens of species that make their homes only in the prairies.

Birds of the prairies

A multitude of birds live in the great grasslands extending across the middle of the continent. Birds of prey glide over the prairies, using their sharp eyes to search for food, while other hunters live within the cover of the low plants and tallgrasses looking for insects and other animal life. Still other birds depend on a harvest of seeds and fruits.

For many people, the bird that best symbolizes the prairie is the meadowlark. Both eastern and western meadowlarks abound, filling the grasslands with their glorious song. The dickcissel, a bird that resembles a miniature meadowlark, has a black bib on a yellow breast (in the male) and lives in the hayfields and abandoned weed patches of the open countryside.

The ring-necked pheasant, an introduced species that has adapted to living with man, sometimes nesting in the suburbs of large cities, claims the central plains as its most successful habitat—and is being blamed by some naturalists for pushing out native species. The birds can often be seen in cornfields and hedgerows. Ring-necked pheasants are large birds with long, pointed tails. The male has a distinct white ring around its neck.

One of the showiest prairie birds is the greater prairie chicken, a bird that resembles a chicken but, when it comes to courtship, is far more interesting. To attract females, the male prairie chicken inflates orange sacs on his neck, and black horn-like tufts of feathers appear on the heads of both sexes. The male's elaborate courtship dance has inspired some of the dances of Native American plains tribes. These birds live on the tallgrass prairie.

Larger than a house sparrow, the bobolink originally came from the prairie grasslands and spread as far east as New England during the peak era of agricultural clearing. Now, though, with so many abandoned farms, it is once again retreating to the central states. Bobolinks resemble sparrows in summer and fall, with buff-colored breasts and brown stripes on the wings and back. But in spring, the males sport a black breast and head, and a back which is a mixture of buff, white, and black. Bobolinks are noted for their bubbly song. The lark bunting is another abundant prairie bird and resembles the spring bobolink.

And among the less common birds are the pipit, the longspur, many species of sparrow—including the clay-colored sparrow—and the sandhill crane, a now-famous bird of marshes and bogs that is continually losing ground as its habitat disappears. Besides the red-tailed hawk, the dominant birds of prey are the ferruginous hawk and the Swainson's hawk, both about red-tailed size.

Prairie dogs live in the dry short-grass prairies of the West. They dig elaborate systems of tunnels that serve both as protection from predators and places to raise young.

Prairie mammals

The mammals of the prairie include the white-tailed deer, coyote (now a frequent resident in states as far east as New York and Massachusetts), both red and gray foxes, striped skunk (and to a lesser degree, eastern spotted skunk), badger, long-tailed weasel, bog lemming, meadow jumping mouse, least shrew, eastern mole, woodchuck, fox squirrel, prairie dogs of the shortgrass prairie, and, of course, the mighty bison that once not only roamed the Great Plains but ranged as far east as the coast and as far south as South Carolina.

Beautiful butterflies

The wildflowers of the prairie grassland also serve as home to a wonderful collection of butterflies and moths, including the beautiful buckeye, the meadow fritillary, the American painted lady, the viceroy, and the monarch. Perhaps the most striking of the many prairie butterflies is the lovely orange-bordered blue, which counts alfalfa (*Medicago sativa*), Lambert locoweed (*Oxytropis lambertii*), and lupines (*Lupinus* spp.) among its host plants.

Meadow and prairie gardens are heaven for butterflies. Here an American painted lady rests on the fluffy white blossoms of meadowsweet (*Spiraea latifolia*).

Prairie plants

The great Dust Bowl of the 1930's was created by farmers who stripped the prairie of all natural vegetation in order to plow the rich soil for crops. The result was an erosion disaster. Before this land was tilled, however, most of it was covered with beautiful and useful annual and perennial wildflowers and grasses that bound the soil together. Luckily, many of them are available today either from seed or as plants.

Prairie grasses provide cover for all sorts of mammals, and are also nest sites for birds. The seedheads of grasses are an important food source for birds as well. The dozens of grass species found growing wild across the prairies of America fall into two broad categories: warm-season and cool-season grasses.

Warm-season grasses stay green and grow actively during the summer but become dormant when temperatures are cool. In fall, their green color changes to tan and brown. Seeds of warm-season grasses can be planted at any time in spring or summer, until about two months before the first killing frost of fall; the seeds must have warm soil for germination. These grasses are very drought-resistant. Except for the fescues and sweet grass, the prairie grasses that follow are all warm-season grasses. All are beneficial to wildlife and could be grown in a prairie habitat garden.

Cool-season grasses begin to grow early in the spring, become dormant during the hot months of summer, and then green up again in the fall. The only way to keep them green in summer is to give them plenty of water. But when you're growing them in a prairie garden with lots of other plants, it's perfectly fine to let them go dormant—the other plants will cover for them. In most of the country, plant these grasses in early spring or early fall. In hot climates, plant the grasses in spring, fall, or winter.

Good grasses for meadow and prairie gardens include big bluestem (*Andropogon gerardii*), little bluestem (*Schizachyrium scoparium*), blue gramma grass (*Bouteloua gracilis*), sweet grass (*Hierochloe odorata*), switchgrass (*Panicum virgatum*), Indian grass (*Sorghastrum nutans*), prairie cordgrass (*Spartina pectinata*), prairie dropseed (*Sporobolus heterolepis*), and buffalo grass (*Buchloë dactyloides*). All are readily available from nurseries, most in either seed or plant form. See "Prairie and meadow grasses" on the opposite page for descriptions.

Little bluestem (*Schizachyrium scoparium*) is an excellent grass for a prairie garden. The state grass of Nebraska, little bluestem is found in the wild in mixed and shortgrass prairies. In autumn, the leaves turn a warm reddish brown color.

Prairie and meadow grasses

Blue gramma grass (*Bouteloua gracilis*), 18–24 inches tall, a foot taller when in flower. Native to the High Plains. Fine-textured and low-growing; purple fall foliage color; silvery, caterpillar-like seedheads. It can either be mowed two or three times a year or left alone. Especially beautiful when dotted with wildflowers. Zones 2–10, shortgrass prairie.

Bluestem, big (*Andropogon gerardii*), 4–6 feet tall. Blue-green to silver-blue foliage; purplish flower spikes in late summer to early fall. Plants turn light reddish brown after the first frost and persist in very cold landscapes until bent over and covered by snow. Zones 4–10, tallgrass and mixed prairies.

Bluestem, little (*Schizachyrium scoparium*, formerly *Andropogon scoparius*), 2–3 feet tall. Pale green foliage turns a golden reddish brown in the fall; small but attractive flowers in summer mature to fluffy seedheads. State grass of Nebraska. Often seen in abandoned fields and along roadsides where it was once planted for soil conservation. Zones 3–10, mixed and shortgrass prairies.

Buffalo grass (*Buchloë dactyloides*), about 6 inches tall. A fine alternative to regular lawn grasses; does not need mowing and tolerates poor soil. Doesn't do well in competition with other prairie grasses and must be watered in dry summers to stay green. Zones 3–9, shortgrass prairie.

Indian grass (*Sorghastrum nutans*), 2–3 feet tall; 5–8 feet tall in flower. Forms golden, plumelike seedheads in September; burnt orange fall color. One of the most beautiful grasses. Zones 4–9, mixed or shortgrass prairies.

Prairie cordgrass (*Spartina pectinata*), 3–6 feet tall (below). Blades ripple, wave, and fold like fanciful ribbons in a light breeze. Flower spikes open above foliage in July; golden fall color. Does well in sandy, heavy, wet, or dry soils. Zones 4–9, tallgrass prairies.

Prairie dropseed (*Sporobolus heterolepis*), about 2 feet tall. Clumps of extremely fine, arching foliage; showy sead heads in late summer; turns golden yellow in the fall and fades to creamy white for winter. Zones 3–9, mixed or shortgrass prairies.

Sweet grass (*Hierochloe odorata*), about 1–3 feet tall. Smells of vanilla and has long been used in making baskets or as incense. Bronze flower panicles in late spring and early summer. Plants need extra water during hot summers. Releases a pleasant odor when crushed. Zones 2–6, tallgrass prairie.

Switchgrass (*Panicum virgatum*), 4–7 feet tall. Beautiful, feathery seedheads; upright clumps turn a lovely orange-yellow in fall and hold their form over winter. Zones 5–9, mixed and shortgrass prairies.

Prairie cordgrass

Prairie wildflowers

FLOWERS FOR TALLGRASS OR SHORTGRASS PRAIRIES:

Anise hyssop, lavender hyssop (*Agastache foeniculum*), 2–3 feet tall. Fragrant leaves; purple flower spikes. A particular favorite of bees and butterflies. Zones 5–9.

Black-eyed Susan (*Rudbeckia hirta*), 1–3 feet tall (below). Coarse, oblong leaves; many 2- to 3-inch golden yellow daisy-like flowers with purple-brown centers borne in summer. A tough, drought-tolerant, long-blooming plant that thrives in hot weather. Plants are short-lived perennials grown as annuals.

Butterfly weed (*Asclepias tuberosa*), 1–3 feet tall. Lance-shaped leaves; flat clusters of brilliant orange flowers in summer. Drought-resistant. Attracts all sorts of butterflies and hummingbirds. Zones 3–9.

Flowering spurge (*Euphorbia corollata*), 1–3 feet tall. Pale green leaves, clusters of white flowers in summer. Zones 3–8.

Black-eyed Susan

Gray-headed coneflower (*Ratibida pinnata*), 4–5 feet tall. Lance-shaped leaves; midsummer down-turned daisy-like flowers of bright yellow. Zones 3–9.

Lance-leaved coreopsis (*Coreopsis lanceolata*), 1–2 feet tall. Dark green lance-shaped leaves; bright yellow daisy-like flowers. Blooms in late spring and summer. Zones 3–8.

Leadplant (*Amorpha canescens*), 2–3 feet tall. Fuzzy gray-green leaves; tiny, purple flowers on 6-inch spikes in late summer and fall. A shrubby legume that fixes nitrogen. A butterfly favorite. Zones 2–7.

Pale purple coneflower (*Echinacea pallida*), 3–5 feet tall. Lance-shaped leaves; daisy-like flowers with drooping pale lavender petals and orange cone-shaped centers in summer. Zones 4–8.

Showy goldenrod (*Solidago speciosa*), 1–3 feet tall. Slender, bright green, lance-shaped leaves; fountains of brilliant yellow flowers in fall. Attracts butterflies. Zones 5–9.

Spiderwort (*Tradescantia ohiensis*), 1–3 feet tall (opposite). Grass-like long, narrow, blue-green leaves; in late spring and early summer, deep blue flowers bloom on each plant, lasting only for a day. Zones 3–9.

Spotted Joe-Pye weed (*Eupatorium maculatum*), 4–8 feet tall. Dark green whorled leaves; large clusters of pale purple to cherry-red flowers in summer and fall. Beloved by swallowtail butterflies. Zones 2–8.

White false indigo (*Baptisia alba*), 2–3 feet tall. Oblong to lance-shaped leaves, 1–2 inches long; spikes of pea-like white flowers in early summer. Zones 5–8.

FLOWERS FOR TALLGRASS PRAIRIES:

Compass plant (*Silphium laciniatum*), 8–10 feet tall. Dozens of daisy-like yellow flowers cover the plant in late summer; particularly likes moist soil. Birds relish the seeds. Zones 5–9.

Greenheaded coneflower (*Rudbeckia laciniata*), 2½–6 feet tall. Large, lobed leaves; 2- to 3-inch yellow daisy-like flowers with drooping petals and green centers in late summer. Zones 3–9.

New England aster (*Aster novae-angliae*), 3–6 feet tall. Small, narrow leaves; small, star-like flowers in bright blue, rose, violet, or even magenta, depending on the cultivar, with yellow-orange centers. Blooms in late summer. A butterfly plant. Zones 3–8.

Prairie blazing-star (*Liatris pycnostachya*), 3–5 feet tall. Large, strap-like foliage; large, showy spikes of rose-purple flowers in midsummer. Attracts butterflies and hummingbirds. Zones 3–9.

Purple coneflower (*Echinacea purpurea*), 2–4 feet tall. Shrubby plants with oval leaves; large, long-lasting, daisy-like purple-pink flowers with stiff orange to brown centers, in mid-to-late summer. A butterfly plant; birds eat the seeds. Zones 3–8.

Queen-of-the-prairie (*Filipendula rubra*), 4–6 feet tall. Compound leaves; large, feathery clusters of tiny pink flowers resembling cotton candy in late spring and summer. Tolerates moist soil. Zones 3–9.

Rattlesnake master (*Eryngium yuccifolium*), 2–3 feet tall. Stiff, narrow leaves; flower stalks up to 6 feet tall with green, thistle-like flowers, more unusual than beautiful. Blooms in summer and fall. Zones 4–9.

Sunflower heliopsis (*Heliopsis helianthoides*), 3–5 feet tall. Bushy, with dark green triangular leaves; 2- to 3-inch yellow daisy-like flowers in July. Zones 3–9.

Wild bergamot (*Monarda fistulosa*), 2–5 feet tall. Mint-like foliage; lavender or pink mop-head flowers in summer. Beloved of bees and butterflies. Zones 3–9.

FLOWERS FOR SHORTGRASS PRAIRIES:

Azure aster (*Aster azureus*), 2–3 feet tall. Oblong leaves; bright blue daisy-like flowers. Attractive to butterflies. Zones 3–8.

Large-flowered beardtongue (*Penstemon grandiflorus*), 3–4 feet tall. Upright; oval blue-green leaves; 2-inch lavender flowers like snapdragons in early summer. A hummingbird plant. Zones 3–8.

Rocky Mountain blazing-star (*Liatris ligulistylis*), 2–3 feet tall. Large, oblong leaves; brilliant purple flowers in summer. Attractive to butterflies and hummingbirds. Zones 3–8.

Spiderwort

The prairie tapestry

If you think prairies and meadows are dull and limited to green, think again. Over, under, and through all these grasses are found a host of lovely wildflowers. Wildflowers are an important part of a prairie habitat. The blossoms attract butterflies, moths, and bees; the seedheads provide food for birds.

Whether you plant a tallgrass, shortgrass, or mixed prairie garden will depend on where you live and what the growing conditions are like. Wildflowers for all types of prairie gardens include butterfly weed (*Asclepias tuberosa*), lavender or anise hyssop (*Agastache foeniculum*), leadplant (*Amorpha canescens*), lance-leaved coreopsis (*Coreopsis lanceolata*), pale purple coneflower (*Echinacea pallida*), Joe-Pye weed (*Eupatorium fistulosum*), flowering spurge (*Euphorbia corollata*), black-eyed Susan (*Rudbeckia hirta*), showy goldenrod (*Solidago speciosa*), and spiderworts (*Tradescantia* spp.). Among the best plants for a tallgrass prairie garden are purple coneflower (*Echinacea purpurea*), rattlesnake master (*Eryngium yuccifolium*), queen-of-the-prairie (*Filipendula rubra*), prairie blazing-star (*Liatris pycnostachya*), bergamot (*Monarda didyma*), yellow coneflower (*Ratibida columnifera*), green-headed coneflower (*Rudbeckia laciniata*), compass plant (*Silphium laciniatum*), New England aster (*Aster novae-angliae*), and sunflower heliopsis (*Heliopsis helianthoides*). Good choices for a shortgrass prairie include azure aster (*Aster azureus*), Rocky Mountain blazing-star (*Liatris ligulistylus*), and beardtongues (*Penstemon* spp.). These plants are described in "Prairie wildflowers" on page 68.

When the wildflowers are in bloom, the prairie becomes a tapestry of color. Here, asters are in bloom as far as the eye can see on a Colorado shortgrass prairie.

Creating meadow and prairie gardens

Whether you plan on creating a meadow garden, a prairie garden, or a garden devoted to prairie grasses, the same rules of site preparation apply.

Whatever garden you choose, there are two important things to remember: First, prairie grasses need full sun to thrive. If your site is shaded, do not use these grasses. Instead try a combination of red fescue (*Festuca rubra*) and side oats gramma grass (*Bouteloua curtipendula*).

Second, remember that perennial meadow wildflowers and virtually all prairie plants need two to three years to become established, and in the case of prairie plants, because of their deep root systems. During the first year of growth most of the plants' energies are directed to the growing roots. After all, it's those deep root systems that guaranteed survival from the vast prairie fires that once raged across the landscape. So don't expect instant results, and do expect to do some weeding.

Soil preparation is the next most important factor in preparing these gardens. The seedbed must be smooth and weed free. We must underscore this point: Unless this procedure is followed, only failure will result. Existing weeds, many of which are aliens brought over from Europe, will always compete with prairie grasses, meadow grasses, and wildflowers for water, sunlight, and nutrients. If these weeds are allowed to grow unchecked, they will eventually take over your garden and you'll be left with a sorry sight.

A smooth, well-prepared seedbed will lead to quick germination of the seeds you plant. Even if you are transplanting mature plants rather than sowing seed, the same rules apply.

Site preparation

After you've chosen the place for your new garden, the first step is preparing the soil, which means removing all the existing vegetation. Although on large plots of land this can be a daunting task, with backyard gardens it is much easier to achieve. All existing plants—whether grass or weeds—can be smothered without the use of any herbicides.

You merely cover the ground with sheets of black plastic, pieces of old plywood (usually in 4- by 8-foot sheets), or even layers of newspapers or leaves. Alternatively, you can "solarize" the weeds by covering them with clear plastic, a method that cooks plants, speeds germination, then bakes the seedlings. Whatever kind of cover you use, begin the process in late spring and leave the covering in place for two months or more.

When the plants are dead, remove the covering and let everything dry. Then the soil can be easily tilled and the vegetation plowed under.

Persistent weeds

Even though all the existing plants have been plowed under to eventually add organic matter to the soil, weed seeds will remain. If allowed to germinate, they will immediately compete with—and in many cases overtake—your wildflowers and grasses.

So after the initial preparation is finished, give those remaining weed seeds a chance to germinate. Wait about a week after a good soaking rain (or a heavy sprinkling), then till the soil to a depth of 1 inch. This will kill the existing weed seedlings that responded to the water, but won't unearth those that still lurk at a greater depth.

Exchanging lawns for meadows

The easiest way to prepare an existing lawn for a prairie or meadow garden is to rent a sod cutter and use it to remove the top 3 inches of grass and soil. Then prepare the soil and plant the area immediately, remembering that the new garden will always be lower than the surrounding land. You can buy new soil to replace what has been taken away, but make sure you purchase good soil rather than common fill, which can be contaminated, full of weeds and debris, or heavy clay subsoil.

Another way to clear out the grass is by cultivation. This means digging up the soil with a tiller at least twice, with the sessions spaced about a week apart. If rhizomatous perennial grasses have been used in your lawn, it may take up to a year to eliminate them completely.

Establishing a meadow garden

It would be wonderful if wildlife gardeners could collect their own seed for planting a meadow garden, but in today's world most people just don't have the time. However, before you buy a wildflower seed mix, contact your state or local native plant society and your local county Cooperative Extension agent to learn about any invasive plants in your area that should not be planted in your garden.

There are different wildflower seed assortments available for different kinds of meadow gardens. Among the choices are annual wildflowers, perennial wildflowers, moist meadow mixes, dry land mixes for areas where water is scarce, and mixes specifically for different climates and areas of the country. There are even mixes especially designed to attract birds and butterflies.

Beware of "instant meadow" seed mixes that promise dazzlingly colorful results. They contain mostly annuals and nonnative garden flowers that are not likely to come back next year. These mixes often contain western flowers that will not reseed outside their native habitats. Unless you plan to overseed or reseed your meadow every year, avoid these tempting offers. See "Resources for wildlife gardeners" on page 187 for suppliers of meadow seed mixes.

When sowing newly turned land, most reliable seed companies suggest using 10 pounds of seed per acre (5 pounds of grass seed and 5 pounds of wildflower seed). If the land already has existing trees and shrubs, 5 pounds of seed per acre is suggested.

To create tightly packed growth, gardeners can use up to 15 pounds per acre on flat land and up to 20 pounds on steep slopes. The average city lot of 50 by 150 feet needs about 1½ pounds of seed. For most gardens in the United States, the best time to sow a meadow or prairie garden is spring.

Broadcast seeding

Broadcast seeding is the same technique used for seeding lawns. On small areas, you can broadcast seed by hand. First mix the seed with a

When planting a meadow garden, it is essential to choose a seed mix suited to your region and to the growing conditions on your property.

lightweight but inert material like vermiculite or untreated sawdust that has been dampened so the seed will stick to it. This helps to mix the seed—especially the smaller varieties—and allows you to see where you've been as you sow.

For a 1,000-square-foot area you will need about two-thirds of a bushel basket of inert material. Mix the seed evenly through the material, then take one-half of the mix and spread it over the area by throwing the mix out with your hand in wide sweeps. After using the first half of the mix, repeat the procedure with the second half, only this time walk in a direction at right angles to your first sweep.

Next, gently rake the seed mix into the tilled soil. Then roll the site with a lawn roller so that the seed is in tight contact with the soil. Never work with wet soil. If it rains while planting, wait for the soil to dry before using the roller.

Mulching your meadow

Once the seed is planted, it's a good idea to add a light covering of clean, weed-free straw to hold in moisture and help with germination. Don't use too much mulch; you should be able to see soil through the straw. And never use field hay—it always contains too many undesirable weeds.

Watering the right way

For the first six weeks after planting, regular watering will not only assist seed germination but will also help small seedlings survive until they have adequate root systems. After six weeks, your garden should be all right on its own.

If there is a prolonged season of drought, water the garden, but only in the early morning. With either sprinklers or a hand-held hose, water for only 15 to 30 minutes. Too much water, especially in clay soil, can be harmful to many wildflowers and native grasses, especially those adapted to dry prairie conditions.

Prairie plants, like these purple coneflowers (*Echinacea purpurea*), are adapted to dry conditions, so they don't need much water.

Maintaining a meadow

Most wild perennials are slow to mature. Since most native plants will only reach a height of about 6 inches in their first year after seeding, by cutting the taller weeds back, you kill the weeds but spare the flowers. The best tool is a hand-held weed trimmer. Don't use a rotary lawn mower or a sickle bar mower.

Begin cutting back the weeds when they reach a height of 8 to 12 inches, then return to the garden and cut again every month. This is very important—for when left on their own, weeds will take over and destroy all your work.

At the end of your growing season, stop cutting back the weeds. They can remain over the winter to give some protection to the smaller wildflowers growing in their shadows.

The second spring

When the second year rolls around, before growth resumes in early spring, whatever is left from the first year should be mowed to the ground. This helps in the germination of any seeds left over from the previous year and encourages most of the wildflowers to grow even thicker for the second season. Be sure you gently remove the cuttings with a bamboo rake, being careful not to rake out any seedling plants.

Transplanting wildflowers and grasses

Sometimes mature plants must be moved either to or from a prairie or meadow garden. When transplanting, remember that just like seedlings, plants need a chance to settle in before they can compete with other flowers and grasses—and fight off weedy plants.

When transplanting all but the smallest plants, allow one square foot of area per plant. And make sure you put plants with the same likes and dislikes together. Dig a hole big enough to spread the roots out in, rough up the sides of the hole, stir up the soil, and keep the new plant's crown at the same height as before. Water well, and in time of drought, don't forget to keep watering until the new roots have settled in.

Chapter Five

Water Gardens

Animals of all kinds are drawn to a water garden, whether it is in the city or the countryside. Small insects and mammals can exist on rainwater, puddles, or morning dew, but both they and larger creatures will be attracted to any new source of clean water. Birds will come to bathe on hot days. Squirrels, chipmunks, raccoons, opossums, and other mammals will come to drink and play. Even if you only have room for a simple pool built from a washtub, you can still have a lovely water garden that's visited by an amazing variety of wildlife.

Wetland wildlife

When your garden features a pool or pond, you'll discover all sorts of "neighbors" you never knew you had. In late spring, dragonflies will appear around almost any quiet body of water. These aerial acrobats of the insect world—with wonderful names like the green darner and the circumpolar bluet—provided engineers with the original idea for the helicopter. Like tiny replicas of those machines, they bob up and down, zipping across the water with glistening wings that blur in the sunlight. But these are only the first insects to arrive. Soon, there will also be damselflies, water striders, and a host of brilliant butterflies and moths, all attracted by the water.

Spring peepers, frogs, and more

The spring should also bring a number of amphibians to your water garden. Even as winter exits, the spring peepers and tree frogs will start their lively chorus.

Frogs and toads will lay their long necklaces of eggs in the water, eggs that eventually turn to tadpoles (or polliwogs). You can follow their progress as they spend weeks, or months, swimming about in your pond before changing to their adult form. And along with the frogs, the eastern newts (also called red efts) begin their life as a kind of tadpole, and they, too, will find their way to your backyard.

Close to the water's edge you might be lucky enough to spot one of the fishing spiders, fast-moving members of the spider clan that can catch tiny fish and the small flying insects that frequent the shallow edge of the pond.

Water striders will skate with ease on the pond's surface. Waxy hairs on their feet are impervious to water, allowing these insects to walk on the surface film of the water, the only visible marks being a slight indentation on the water's surface and the shadows they cast on the floor of the pond.

Squirrels, mice, and chipmunks will all drink from your pond and, even in the suburbs, turtles will find their way to the water. Even

If you have a water garden, you will probably have frogs. This green frog has found a seat on a lotus leaf.

beautiful snakes like the rough green snake will be drawn to the water's edge in search of insects.

Birds, bats, and water

Not only in suburban pools and ponds but in city ponds, too, the green heron will walk in the water on its stilt-like legs, its beak ready to spear a meal from the shallows of your pond. In larger ponds, the heron can also be seen walking the water's edge, looking for fish or tadpoles. Kingfishers live beside water, and even hummingbirds will dart down for a quick drink. At dusk, chimney swallows will drift across the water seeking mites and midges, and as the purple of the twilight sky turns to black, small bats will join in the hunt for insects.

Above left: **Dragonflies are the aerial acrobats of the water garden and are fascinating to watch on a summer afternoon. They are quite beautiful, too. This ruby meadowfly was photographed in Massachusetts.**

Above right: **The green-backed heron is drawn to backyard water gardens and can be seen in ponds and pools in suburban and even city locations.**

Providing water

There are a number of water sources possible for the wildlife garden. Gardeners in more rural situations may have a creek or a seasonal stream, while a few fortunate gardeners will live on property that already has a small pond (either natural or artificial) or borders a lake or river. Even if you don't already have water on your property, you can build a small pond using some of the marvelous new pond liners described on page 84. And wildlife gardeners can always provide water for birdbaths, even if they have to take out water in pails or buckets during periods of prolonged dry weather.

✒ Birdbaths, seasonal streams, puddles

In areas of the country where rain is a common occurrence, there is usually enough water around the garden to provide a temporary source for most ground-dwelling animals and insects. But it usually isn't enough for the larger mammals and birds. Running lawn sprinklers is not ecologically sensible (many cities have water rationing during hours of peak demand, when most of the animals need water, too), so we have to look for other, more practical ways of providing water.

Birdbaths provide water for both drinking and bathing. Most birds prefer them raised on a pedestal, but others will use a birdbath on the ground. These young robins are enjoying a dip in a ground-level clay birdbath sheltered by nearby plants.

Puddles are great for attracting some birds, and a number of butter-flies exhibit a behavior called puddling, in which dozens of these winged beauties cluster around an area of damp mud. But such water sources are really too temporary for most wildlife gardens.

One answer is the time-honored birdbath. Place one on a support that keeps it off the ground so birds will feel comparatively safe from predators while drinking and bathing. Place a second birdbath directly on the ground, where most mammals are accustomed to looking for water. A hollowed-out stump or a section of log can hold a waterproof container and make a great birdbath. Even a garbage can lid will hold enough water to attract many animals. (Site it in the shade so the water stays cool.)

One attractive way to satisfy both birds and mammals is to create a split-level water source. Set a birdbath on top of a pile of rocks and feed it with a hidden hose set to dribble water into it. Place a second birdbath a bit lower down, where it can catch the overflow. As the water spills over the rim of the first birdbath, it falls into the other birdbath just below.

An unfrozen source of water is important for wildlife in winter. To use a birdbath heater, you will need a nearby electrical outlet.

Unfrozen water in winter

When winter comes to most parts of the country, water begins to freeze. Water lilies can be lifted from small ponds and stored over the winter, but what can you do to help the wildlife—especially the birds—left outdoors?

One thing you can do is keep the water from freezing. Using a weatherproof extension cord for power, you can tape an aquarium heater in place to prevent the water from getting too cold. Or buy a stock tank heater from a farm supply store. Many nature and bird specialty stores now stock special birdbath heaters to do the job.

If your birdbath has a hollow pedestal, you can install a 60-watt light bulb just below the bath itself, and leave it on whenever the temperature falls below the freezing mark. The heat from the bulb should keep the water liquid. In areas of the country where freezing weather is a rarity, simply put warm water outside every day until the weather warms up again. For larger in-ground pools, there is an automatic pool deicer that uses a thermostat and operates on 110-volt household current. It comes in 1,500 watts for USDA Zone 5 or colder, and 1,000 watts for Zone 6.

Simple water gardens

For those gardeners without a natural source of water nearby, there are other answers to providing for wildlife. You can make a small pool from half of a whiskey barrel or wine keg (either buried or set up on rocks or a low stump), a buried aluminum horse trough, a buried bathtub (its edges hidden by flat rocks), or even a large plastic bucket.

When the tub or other container is in a place where you want it to remain all season, fill it halfway with sandy loam soil. (Do not add compost or other organic matter to the soil; it will cloud the water.) Let water trickle slowly into the container from a hose until the container is a bit more than half full.

Plant a water lily in the center of the tub. Add whatever additional plants you want, finishing off with a couple of bunches of oxygenating plants, such as *Elodea* spp., set near the edge of the tub. When all the plants are in place, fill the container to the top with water, adding it at a slow trickle as before. If you want to introduce a few fish into the water garden, do so a few days later.

This lovely small pond is home to water lilies and a mixed planting of yellow flag iris (*Iris pseudacorus*) and pickerel weed (*Pontederia cordata*). Chinese astilbe (*Astilbe chinensis* var. *pumila*), which likes moist soil, blooms alongside the pool.

Permanent water gardens

For a larger water garden or a more natural look, you can make a pool from a waterproof plastic or rubber liner. Preformed fiberglass pools now come in more natural shapes, too. Even an old leaking concrete pond can be made serviceable again with the addition of a liner. Depending on the size of your wildlife garden, one of these solutions should fit your needs.

Choosing a site

When choosing a site for your backyard pool, remember that a water garden for wildlife is different from one that's meant to add a sophisticated design accent to a lovely garden. Pools added for the use of wildlife are another story. Because of the low volume of water, a small water garden—whether it's intended for wildlife or not—may need shade during the hottest part of the day to prevent the water from becoming overly warm for plants and fish. A water garden designed for aesthetics, however, would likely exclude the presence of overhanging trees in order to cut back on yearly maintenance, especially the need to clean up fallen leaves. A pool created for use of wildlife, on the other hand, would be especially valuable if it had trees nearby to provide cover for creatures wishing to stop by for a drink.

Keep your pool away from areas subject to runoff, especially after hard rains. You may be very careful about the use of pesticides and other chemicals around your home, but you can't always know what your neighbors are using. Lawns are frequently overfertilized and are a major source of water pollution from fertilizer runoff. Even a careless oil spill from somebody changing oil in a car could be carried by running water to a low spot in your yard, where it could harm wildlife using a pool located there.

Since a lot of the pleasure of wildlife gardening comes from watching the wildlife, make sure you site your water garden where you can see it. If you place the pond so that it is visible from part of the house, it will add a lot to the family's enjoyment.

An instant small-space water garden

Many nurseries now stock a freestanding "kettle" made of black plastic that has a 36-inch diameter and holds about 36 gallons of water. When planted with one of the small water lilies (*Nymphaea* spp.), a spike rush (*Eleocharis montevidensis*) or two, a sweet flag (*Acorus calamus*), or common horsetail (*Equisetum hyemale*), even these small water gardens will attract insects, frogs, and birds to the backyard. You can easily add the alluring sound and sight of falling water to this tiny pool by attaching a dripping hose to an overhanging branch, allowing just enough water to continually drip into the water below. Because of its small size and the possibility of the water getting too warm, make sure you site these small pools where they'll be shaded during the heat of the day.

To plant a tiny water garden in a kettle, first fill the container half full with soil (clay loam works best; do not add compost or other organic material, which would turn the water cloudy). Add water at a slow trickle until the kettle is a bit more than half full.

Then put in the plants, beginning in the center of the container and working out toward the edges. In addition to the plants listed above, you may want to add a couple of oxygenating plants such as arrowhead (*Sagittaria graminea*) and waterweeds (*Elodea* spp.).

When all the plants are in place, fill the container to the top with water, again letting it trickle in slowly to avoid disturbing the soil.

The new pond liners

Until twenty years ago, if a homeowner wanted to install a small pool or pond in the backyard, it was an expensive proposition requiring extensive digging, concrete forms, and poured concrete. Then within a few years, the pool would leak, especially in a cold climate.

Since then, some things have changed for the better. When it comes to installing a small pond these days, instead of a great deal of money and a week or more of effort, the project can be accomplished by a family in a single enjoyable weekend.

The invention that transformed the science of pool-building is the flexible pond liner. These waterproof liners, made of polyvinyl chloride (PVC), rubber, or a combination of materials, will last a very long time, usually ten years or longer.

There are three types of liners you can choose for a backyard pond: PVC, rubber, or a product called GeoPond.

The least expensive is the PVC liner. It is usually 20 mils thick, black in color, tear resistant, and has a 5- to 20-year guarantee. A 10-by-15-foot liner makes an 18-inch deep, 6-by-11-foot pool for a cost of about $100. To create a similar-sized pool out of 2-ply PVC liner, which is 32 mils thick and guaranteed for 10 years, would cost $170.

In a shady garden, this tiny, rock-edged pool provides both a home for fish and drinking and bathing water for birds and small mammals.

Rubber liners are 45 mils thick, black, resistant to ultraviolet (UV) light, and have a 20-year lifespan. A 10-by-15-foot liner costs about $150. With either PVC or rubber liners, it is best to first install an underlayer of flexible pond liner. This adds about $35 to the initial cost of each of these liners but protects them from rocks, sticks, and other debris on the pond floor. You can substitute carpeting or a 2-inch layer of sand for the pond liner.

GeoPond liners are made of 32-mil rubber bonded to a layer of 28-mil geotextile fabric. They are very strong (60 mils thick), black, and resistant to ultraviolet light, and their thickness helps to prevent punctures and tearing. These liners are guaranteed for 30 years and run about $300 for a 6-by-11-foot pool. No additional underlayer is needed. They are available from Lilypons Water Gardens, 6800 Lilypons Road, P.O. Box 10, Buckeystown, MD 21717 (catalog $5).

Making a liner pond or pool

Complete installation instructions come with any liner and consist mainly of choosing an outline and excavating the soil 1 to 2 feet deep, a depth sufficient to support both plants and fish. Be careful to remove any stones that could possibly puncture the liner. Next, check to see that the pond is level from edge to edge; use a carpenter's level on a two-by-four. Remove soil from the high spots until the entire bottom of the pond is level. Then add a 1-inch layer of damp sand. If needed, put the underliner in place, then carefully drape the PVC or rubber liner around and into the excavation; it shouldn't be stretched. You will need two people to move and position most liners. The liners will be held in place by the weight of the water they hold. After filling with water, let the pool settle for a day. Then cut the excess liner back, leaving a 6- to 12-inch flap. Nail it into the ground with 10-inch spikes. The pond edges can be hidden by covering them with rocks.

Unless you are working in very rocky soil, your pool can usually be finished in a weekend.

Constructing an artificial pool

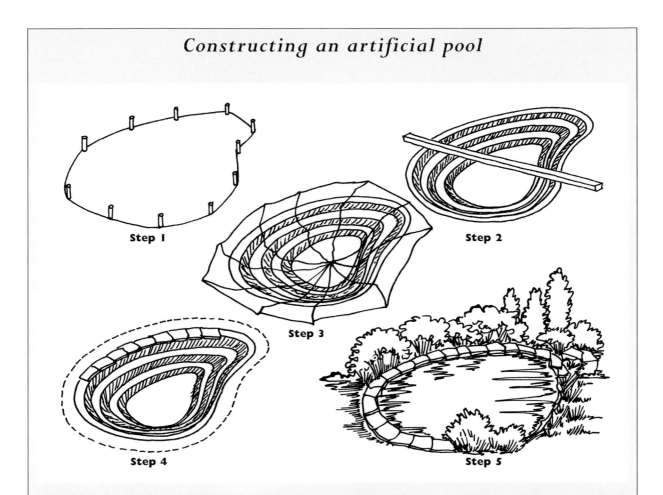

Step 1

Step 2

Step 3

Step 4

Step 5

Step 1 Mark the outline of the pool with stakes and string, and excavate the center to a depth of 1 to 2 feet.

Step 2 Carve terraced ledges in the sides, if desired, and use a carpenter's level on a 2 x 4 to check that the pond is level from edge to edge.

Step 3 Level the bottom of the pool, add 1 inch of damp sand, position the underliner (if you are using one), then drape the pool liner into the hole.

Step 4 Fill the pool with water and let the liner settle for a day. Then cut away the excess liner to leave a 6- to 12-inch flap. Fasten it to the ground and cover with flat stones to hide the edge.

Step 5 Landscape the finished pool by planting around the edges and in containers set on the side ledges and bottom of the pool.

🌿 Preformed pools

There are also various preformed fiberglass pools that come in a number of sizes and shapes, including round, oval, kidney-shaped, and free-form. The smallest measures 3 by 4 feet, holds about 70 gallons of water, and costs around $200, while the largest measures about 14 by 17 feet, holds 600 gallons of water, and costs around $1,000. The advantages are mainly in the life span—a typical fiberglass pond will last about 50 years.

Here's how to install a preformed pool liner. First, it's a good idea to wash the liner to remove any residues that might harm plants or fish. Wash the liner with soapy water (use dishwashing liquid or other mild detergent), then rinse well with clear water.

If there is grass growing on the site where the pool will be, remove it. Cut down into the sod with a sharp spade to outline patches of grass, then push the spade horizontally under the sod and lift it away from the soil. (Pile up the sod in an out-of-the-way place and let it decompose into compost.)

When the grass has been cleared, set the pool liner upside down in the location where the pool will be installed. Trace the outline of the liner on the ground with lime, flour, or a length of rope. Then take away the liner.

Excavate the soil inside your outline to a depth of about 12½ inches, or whatever depth is necessary to allow the lip of the pool liner to sit slightly above ground level when the liner is in the hole. Rake the soil smooth. Use a carpenter's level to check that the bottom of the hole is level and even.

Set the liner in the hole (right side up this time) and fill it with water to hold it in position.

Mix some of the soil taken from the hole with water to make mud. Tamp the mud around the edge of the pool so it fits snugly in the hole.

Finally, finish off the edging with flagstones or field stone. Set the stones neatly around the edge of the pool to cover the lip of the liner.

Fill in between the stones with soil or sand, tamping it firmly into place. Anchoring the stone edging in an underlying layer of mortar makes a more stable edging but is not necessary if you don't plan to walk on the stones very often.

Use large stones to hide the edges of a pond liner when you have finished installing it.

✎ Adding plants and fish

If you're using city water to fill a small pond, don't plant your water garden right away. Let the water stand for at least three days once the pond is full so that the chlorine in the water can evaporate. You'll find planting details on page 98.

The next step is to decide if you want goldfish, koi, or other pond fish. The advantages of having fish are that they help keep your water garden free of mosquitoes and algae, and they're fun to watch. The disadvantages are that they can uproot and even eat plants and can muddy the water in the process. But you can prevent a lot of damage by putting a layer of pea gravel over the soil in the container or pool bottom. If you do opt for goldfish, introduce them about two weeks after the pond has been planted. Give them packaged fish food until there are enough insect larvae in the water to support their food needs.

A small waterfall powered by a recirculating pump is a lovely feature in a backyard water garden.

Caring for pools and ponds

Small ponds need more attention from the gardener than large ponds. When there's more water, there's more of a chance for problems to dissipate before they become overwhelming. Outside of the responsibility of removing large leaves and dead plants before they rot or making sure the occasional dead fish is removed, caring for the wildlife pond is not difficult.

Don't worry about green water

Algae is as natural to a pond as rain is to a summer storm. Every new pond will soon gather algae. When ponds are new, algae is the dominant plant, but as fish and other aquatic creatures reach a balance, the water will start to clear. Don't be upset about the lack of crystal-clear water because water that is clear is dead water. A healthy pond will always have tiny freshwater plankton consisting of protozoa and algae suspended in the water.

The goal in a pond for wildlife is to maintain a balance. A well-balanced pond contains plants that absorb carbon dioxide and release oxygen (a great deal of oxygen is also absorbed through the water's surface). It also contains fish, which take in oxygen and release carbon dioxide. The fish also eat algae, while small insects and animals such as tadpoles and water snails, and the larger protozoa vacuum the bottom of the pond while scavenging for food.

Submerged plants (ones that grow entirely underwater) oxygenate the water in aquariums, and will perform the same function in a small backyard water garden. Two readily available plants to use are water milfoils (*Myriophyllum* spp., hardy in Zones 4–10) and waterweed (*Elodea canadensis*, hardy in Zones 5–10). You will need two or three bunches of plants for each square yard of water surface the pool covers.

Plant the plants in pots of heavy or dense soil. Use clay loam or other soil containing a substantial amount of clay; avoid soil rich in organic matter and potting soils that contain vermiculite or perlite, which will float out of the pot.

When planting has been completed, cover the soil surface in each pot with a layer of pebbles or gravel, and submerge the pots one at a time, setting them on the bottom of the pool. Wait a few weeks until the plants have rooted before adding fish or tadpoles to the pool. Every two years, drain the pool and clean up the muck on the bottom to prevent any unpleasant odors from building up.

Preparations for winter

Deeper ponds can be left alone over the winter as long as the pond bottom is below the frost line. If you don't know how deep frost penetrates in your area, check with your local county Cooperative Extension agent. Fish can live in the pond throughout the winter as long as part of the water is unfrozen; but, contrary to common belief, they cannot spend the winter frozen and revive again in the spring. If your pond is shallow and you cannot take the fish indoors for the winter, be sure to break the ice every day as it forms, or use a stock tank deicer or one of the other water heaters mentioned on page 81 to keep the pond from freezing solid.

If the ice freezes deeper than just a thin skin before you can break it up, you would do better to thaw it with a pond deicer. If you try to break it up yourself, sharp chunks of ice could tear the pool liner.

If your water garden includes some hardy water lilies (*Nymphaea* spp.), you can leave them in the garden in locations where the water will not freeze solid in winter. But if you live in Zone 5 or farther north, where the pool is likely to freeze to the bottom, hardy water lilies should come out of the garden in winter.

After you have experienced a few hard freezes in fall, pull the pots of water lilies out of the pool. Cut off the topgrowth, then wrap the pots in wet newspaper and enclose them in plastic bags. Put the bags in a location (such as an unheated basement or garage) where temperatures stay above freezing but below 40°F. When the pool thaws in spring, the pots of water lilies can go back into the garden.

Bogs and marshes

It is not necessary to install a pond in order to bring the joys of water to your wildlife garden. Here's one case where gardeners with low, damp areas, poorly drained clay soil, or gardens in areas where the water table is close to the surface have the easiest job. Still, if your soil is well-drained, those same PVC and rubber liners used to make ponds can also turn an area of land into a place that will be boggy and wet—without having some of the maintenance problems associated with open water.

Creating a wetland

The concept behind creating a wetland is the same as that of building a pool, only in this case the earth is excavated to a depth of about 12 to 16 inches. After the liner is put in place, punch small holes in the liner, about one for every square yard of material. This allows some of the water to escape slowly. Without this safety valve, you will create a mud hole, not a bog garden.

Before replacing the soil, put in a piece of plastic pipe with holes punched in the top about every 18 inches for drainage. Lay the pipe at the back of the bog garden and on top of the liner. The pipe should extend out into a trench dug in the land behind the future bog. You can cover the pipe with stones to camouflage it. This extra drain also keeps the bog from becoming a muddy soup in times of heavy rain. Once you have laid the pipe, replace the soil and cut away the excess liner. You can use flat stones or rocks to finish the edges. Usually rainfall is enough to keep the soil constantly wet (obviously, if you live in a dry climate it would make little sense to try to establish a bog garden). But if you have an unusually hot summer with reduced rainfall, the bog garden can be brought back to normal dampness with the garden hose.

After you have installed the liner and created your "mini-wetland," observe it for several days to make sure the area is remaining consistently wet. If it dries out, you might not have chosen the right location for a bog garden after all.

Cinnamon fern (*Osmunda cinnamomea*) and skunk cabbage (*Symplocarpus foetidus*) can often be found in wet places along the edges of a woodland or growing beside a shady stream.

Plants for pond and bog

<table>
<tr><td>

**Showy perennials
for the
water's edge**

Blue flag iris (*Iris versicolor*), 1½–3 feet tall. Narrow sword-shaped leaves; beardless blue-violet flowers splashed with yellow in mid-spring to early summer. Zones 4–9.

Japanese iris (*I. ensata*), to 2½ feet tall. Sword-shaped leaves; beardless flowers of reddish purple, white, blue, purple, pink, and other colors, broader than most iris flowers, in June and July. Zones 4–9.

Marsh marigold (*Caltha palustris*), 1–3 feet tall. Heart-shaped green leaves; yellow buttercup-like flowers in spring. Cultivar 'Flore Pleno' has double flowers. Zones 2–8.

Spotted Joe-Pye weed (*Eupatorium maculatum*), 4–6 feet tall. Coarse leaves to 1 foot long; clusters of rose-purple flowers in summer. Zones 2–8.

</td></tr>
</table>

After your pond, pool, or bog is finished, it's time for planting. If nature is left to its own devices, eventually seeds brought by the wind or by birds will bring plants to your watery domain. But nature often takes its time. And when you choose your own plants, you can include plants especially attractive to wildlife.

Foliage plants for the water's edge

The area between a pond or stream and the dry upland is especially attractive to a number of plants and shrubs. And it is here that large-leaved plants offer maximum shelter to animals and insects. Among the large-leaved plants that grow well at the water's edge are the larger species and cultivars of hosta (*Hosta* spp.), which can form mounds of leaves about 2 feet wide and 14 inches tall. Gardeners in Zone 7 or warmer can grow the magnificent gunnera (*Gunnera manicata*), with enormous leaves that can reach 8 to 10 feet across and offer shelter not to just one duck but to a whole flock.

In colder areas, substitute the beautiful maple- or buckeye-leaved rodgersias (*Rodgersia* spp.). Hardy to Zone 4, rodgersias have handsome crinkled leaves that are green, bronze, or purple, and bear plumes of white or pink astilbe-like flowers in late spring or early summer. The Japanese butterbur (*Petasites japonicus*) forms clumps 6 feet tall, is hardy to Zone 5, and has yellow flowers in April and May that are magnets for bees, as well as leaves that offer a layer of protection to small and large animals. And we should certainly mention prairie dock (*Silphium terebinthinaceum*), a large and stately plant, which may reach 10 feet tall with panicles of 3-inch yellow daisy-like flowers in late summer. It is hardy to Zone 4.

Nothing is finer in a water garden than royal fern (*Osmunda regalis*), hardy to Zone 3, and ostrich ferns (*Matteuccia pensylvanica* and *M. struthiopteris*), both hardy to Zone 2. Both have large fronds (ostrich ferns to 9 feet and royal fern to 6 feet long) and provide a shady spot along the edge of a pond or stream.

Even though they all bloom, we usually think of ornamental grasses as foliage plants. Among the best for water gardens is narrow-leaved cotton grass *(Eriophorum angustifolium)*, which is perfect for bog-like conditions or for the edge of the pond. Hardy to Zone 4, it grows 1 to 1½ feet tall with cottonball-like blooms in spring. Variegated manna grass *(Glyceria maxima* 'Variegata'), with its 2- to 3-foot stems of yellow-white, green-striped foliage, brings a beautiful diversity of colors to the water's edge. It is hardy to Zone 5. But for a place for wildlife to hide, for birds to fly about, and for insects to perch, nothing beats prairie cordgrass *(Spartina pectinata)* at the water's edge, or one of the large cultivars of Eulalia grass *(Miscanthus sinensis)*, such as zebra grass *(M. sinensis* 'Zebrinus'), with its yellow-banded foliage, or maiden grass *(M. sinensis* 'Gracillimus'). Prairie cordgrass has arching 3- to 6-foot leaves that turn brilliant gold in fall; it is hardy to Zone 4. The maiden grasses form tall (5- to 6-foot), handsome clumps of foliage and bear showy flower plumes in September; they are hardy to Zone 5.

Japanese primroses (*Primula japonica*) flourish in the moist soil along the edge of a pond or stream.

Cattails (*Typha latifolia*) and a varie-gated cultivar of yellow flag (*Iris pseudacorus* 'Variegata') grow together in a shallow pool.

Flowering plants for the water's edge

Both the common skunk cabbage (*Symplocarpus foetidus*) and yellow skunk cabbage (*Lysichiton americanum*) bloom very early in the spring. The common species has strange brown flowers and a "skunky" odor (it's pollinated by beetles) and the western type has prettier flowers and a strong odor that is unobjectionable to all but the most delicate noses. The bold, upright, cabbage-like foliage adds a handsome accent to a water garden—and luckily, it doesn't smell. Marsh marigold (*Caltha palustris*) has charming waxy yellow flowers, and will grow in shallow water or damp soil.

Japanese iris (*Iris ensata*) and yellow flag (*I. pseudacorus*) are both attractive plants for boggy locations, and their sword-shaped leaves provide plenty of wildlife cover. Spotted Joe-Pye weed (*Eupatorium maculatum*), which grows well in average garden soil, will also thrive in wetlands. Except for butterfly bushes (*Buddleia* spp.) or Mexican sun-flowers (*Tithonia* spp.), no plant collects butterflies like the flat, rose-purple flower heads of the spotted Joe-Pye weed.

Plants for shallow water

Once out into the water, there are still flowering plants that provide food, flowers, and cover. The leaves of the sweet flag (*Acorus calamus*) or those of yellow flag (*Iris pseudacorus*) are favorites of dragonfly nymphs, which live on them during their metamorphosis into adults. The common arrowhead (*Sagittaria latifolia*) and the pickerelweed (*Pontederia cordata*) produce attractive lovely flowers for butterflies.

A few grasses, including manna grass (*Glyceria maxima* 'Variegata') and prairie cordgrass (*Spartina pectinata*), can be planted directly in water. In small ponds, wild rice (*Zizania aquatica*) can either be planted in submerged pots or sown directly in the water. Other water plants like cattails (*Typha* spp.), horsetails (*Equisetum* spp.), and most of the sedges and rushes (*Carex* and *Juncus* spp., respectively) will do well in shallow water. But be warned: Cattails, especially, have a tendency to

Perennial choices for shallow water

Arrowhead (*Sagittaria latifolia*), to 4 feet tall. Arrow-shaped leaves; white flowers with three petals in summer. Zones 5–10.

Pickerelweed (*Pontederia cordata*), 2½ to 4 feet tall. Heart-shaped to lance-shaped leaves.; blue-violet flowers borne on tall stems all summer. Zones 4–9.

Scouring rush horsetail (*Equisetum hyemale*), 1–6 feet tall.

Plants have hollow, jointed evergreen stems without leaves or flowers. The bold green, striped stems add a dramatic touch to the garden. Plant in pots to keep from spreading. Zones 4–10.

Soft rush (*Juncus effusus*), 1½–2½ feet tall. Clumps of rounded, narrow leaves; small green to tan flowers similar to those of grasses. Zones 4–9.

Sweet flag (*Acorus calamus*), 3–6 feet tall. Sword-like leaves; small greenish flowers in spring and summer. 'Variegatus' has yellow-striped leaves . Zones 4–10.

Yellow flag (*Iris pseudacorus*), 3–4 feet tall. Narrow, sword-shaped leaves; beardless yellow flowers in May and June. Cultivar 'Variegata' has handsome, yellow-striped leaves. Zones 4–9.

invade. Cattails will speed up the process of turning a small pond into dry land because, when left unchecked, they soon form a solid sheet of plants. On the other hand, when kept in check, cattails are favorites of a number of shore birds, and down at the water level, they're a preferred hideout for a large number of water animals and insects. The small cattail *T. laxmannii* is better for a small pool, but it's still invasive.

So unless you are planting a small pond where you can weed out invasive plants, if you're growing any of these plants in the water, it's a good idea to plant them in submersible containers. A container will keep them from spreading out of control. For smaller plants in smaller pots, simply set the pots on top of submerged bricks or concrete blocks to bring them up to the correct level in the water.

One of the few grass-like plants you can grow in shallow water without its becoming a pest is the soft rush (*Juncus effusus*). The thick and spiky silhouette is always welcome in the garden, but it's doubly impressive when seen at the water's edge. It's just as effective in pots. It's also a favorite resting spot for dragonflies. Horsetails, while invasive, are great perches for waterside insects as well.

Water lilies and lotuses

Water lily pads in a pond seem to draw frogs like a magnet. And if things look busy on top of these paddle-shaped leaves, you should see what is going on underneath. For years, only large ponds had enough water surface to support these lilies, but today there are many smaller cultivars available. You can even plant miniature cultivars in half-barrels.

Some water lilies can withstand cold weather and are known as hardy water lilies *(Nymphaea* spp.). These perennials have rounded leaves of shiny green, sometimes mottled with reds and burgundies. Some cultivars, like the fragrant white 'Gladstoniana', can be grown in water 3 feet deep, while others, like the white 'Walter Pagels', will do well in a large container. In addition to white, there are pink, red, and yellow flowers. All these water lilies bloom during the day.

Other *Nymphaea* cultivars include the night- and day-blooming tropical water lilies that, outside of Zones 9 and 10, must be brought in for the winter or treated as annuals. Because of their fragrance, the night-bloomers are especially valuable for the moths they attract on warm summer nights. There are tropical water lily cultivars for large ponds, medium or small pools, or even containers.

Nelumbo lutea and *N. nucifera* and their cultivars are known as lotuses. The large round leaves stand well above the water's surface and repel water droplets as though they were mercury. The large fragrant pink, white, or yellow flowers bloom for 6 to 8 weeks and attract many insects. Although most cultivars need a large pond, new smaller cultivars are now available.

Planting the right way

When planting any of the water plants, always use heavy garden soil or topsoil without any additions of vermiculite, perlite, or other fillers because they will float to the top and ruin your water garden's good looks. Avoid commercial potting mixes, too, because they may contain fertilizers or chemicals that could harm fish and other wildlife. Organic

Plant water lilies with the crown (the point where roots meet top-growth) even with the soil surface in the pot. To keep the soil from floating out into the water, cover the soil surface with pea gravel after planting.

matter is also undesirable; it will decompose and dirty the water. A dense clay soil is best for planting in water gardens.

If you put all your water garden plants in containers, it will be easy to take them out when it's time to clean the bottom of the pool or to bring tender plants indoors for winter. It also simplifies the task of dividing crowded perennials when that becomes necessary and prevents invasive spreaders, such as horsetail, from taking over the water garden and squeezing out less aggressive plants. Rinse pots before planting.

To prevent muddying up the water when plants are set into pots before going into the pond, cover the soil in the pots with ½ inch of pea gravel or small stones, then saturate with water before gently lowering the pots into the water.

For bog plants, use good garden soil with some humus added. When working with bog plants, be sure to plant them at the same level they were when in the pot.

It is important to set water garden and bog plants in water of the correct depth if they are to grow properly. Follow carefully the depth requirements and planting instructions provided by the nursery when you purchase your plants.

Chapter Six

Gardening for Birds

A garden without wildlife is a silent garden. Beautiful flowers and sparkling fruits and berries begin to look like sterile photos in an expensive book until bees, butterflies, moths, and—most important—birds begin to fly about. Whether they choose your garden for nesting or just for feeding, birds bring movement, color, sound, and sheer entertainment to you and your family.

Popular backyard birds

Of the hundreds of birds that are seen across this country, a few, because of their appearance and antics, have become stars of a backyard devoted to wildlife. Some, like the European starlings, can be more of a nuisance—and a perfect example of the perils of importing new species without proper research. Originally, 100 of these birds were brought to Central Park in the late 1800s, and now they number in the millions. But starlings are the exception. Most backyard visitors are more than welcome and worth many times their weight in food.

Goldfinches are found in much of the United States. The brilliantly colored males are among our most strikingly beautiful birds. In winter, the males lose their sunny yellow color and take on a more sober brown hue.

✒ American goldfinches

The breeding, winter, and permanent ranges of American goldfinches overlap in such a way that the birds are found throughout most of the country. Bright yellow males and olive-brown females fly across the yard or field like a roller coaster with wings. Goldfinches love niger

seeds (remotely related to American thistles). If you offer niger seeds at your feeder, they will visit often. You'll attract goldfinches to your garden if you plant black-eyed Susans (*Rudbeckia fulgida*) and purple coneflower (*Echinacea purpurea*)—they relish the seeds. And they'll often alight on top of a wild thistle blossom (*Cirsium* spp.) that is turning to fluff. Look for lesser and Lawrence's goldfinches joining the American goldfinches at feeders in the western United States.

Dark-eyed juncos

Dark-eyed juncos (also called snowbirds) are ground feeders that often seem to revel in bad weather, undaunted by wind and snow. Although they will come to hanging feeders, they do their best work when seeds, such as white millet, are spread on the ground, on a feeding table 2 or 3 feet above the ground, or directly on the snow.

Song sparrows

Song sparrows are among the most common songbirds in the country. Because of their dull brown and gray feathers, they're easy to overlook until you hear the clear trilling notes of their songs. Each sparrow has its own song. Usually shy feeders, they will dart out for food scattered on the ground or on feeding trays, but spend most of their time making short hops along the edge between the lawn and the shrubs. Song sparrows are easily identified by a dark spot on their streaked breasts.

Mourning doves

Mourning doves are everywhere. Their sorrowful coos are heard throughout the country, while their whirring wings and strutting walk are common sights at most backyard feeders. When you see these birds scratching in the driveway, they're looking for small bits of stone to add to their crops to aid food digestion. Mourning doves are closely related to the larger European introduction, the pigeon or rock dove, most often seen in cities.

You can easily recognize a nuthatch—they love to walk down tree trunks head first and sometimes climb around on branches upside down. This one's the white-breasted nuthatch.

Hummingbirds

Hummingbirds in America are as varied and beautiful as the jewels in a pirate's treasure. With rapidly beating wings, these birds can hover like tiny helicopters in front of tubular flowers (often red or orange), where they eat nectar and tiny insects. Their iridescent feathers can look like gems. It's easy to attract hummers with sugar-water feeders and many types of flowers, including bee balm (*Monarda didyma*) and cardinal flower (*Lobelia cardinalis*). The ruby-throated hummingbird is common in eastern North America, but there are more than a dozen western species. These include the black-chinned hummingbird found from British Columbia south to central Texas, the broad-tailed hummingbird of the Rocky Mountains to southern Arizona and Texas, and the rufous hummingbird of the Pacific Northwest.

Nuthatches

Both white-breasted and red-breasted nuthatches can be found across the United States. Their common name refers to the bird's practice of hacking open tough hulled seeds, but they should probably be called acrobat birds because they excel in walking all over tree branches and trunks, often upside down. These birds are especially fond of suet and sunflower seeds. Two additional species, the brown-headed nuthatch of the Southeast and the pygmy nuthatch of the Rockies, are more sedentary but respond to the same foods.

House wrens

The most common wren is the house wren, a 5-inch bird that is extremely territorial. Once it settles into a nesting area, other birds had better watch out! House wrens are tough little creatures, and their belligerent antics are always fun to watch. They also eat many pests in the garden. Look for the larger, milder-mannered Carolina wren around feeders in the southeastern and south central states. Bewick's wren and the cactus wren generally live farther west.

Gray catbirds

Catbirds are found over two-thirds of the country, but are most common in the East. Their calls include a series of catlike mews. They will often keep company with the gardener, jumping from branch to branch within the safety of shrubbery and thickets. Catbirds can be easily persuaded to visit a feeder or windowsill for a snack of raisins.

American robins

Robins are perhaps the best-known birds, but in their case familiarity has bred nothing but friendship. Although partial to worms in the lawn, robins, when hungry, may take certain foods from feeders. They also love to eat fruit and visit the birdbath.

Other feathered friends

Other common backyard visitors include the startlingly-red northern cardinals, the greedy evening grosbeaks, a host of different woodpeckers, the noisy and clever jays, and the delightful chickadees and titmice. Think of how enjoyable it will be to welcome these and other birds to your backyard! The year or two of effort it takes to transform your garden into a sanctuary will reward you with a lifetime hobby.

Cardinals feed on the ground, often in groups and just before dark. They announce their arrival with clear chirping calls.

Birds eat at varied levels

When planning and planting your bird habitat, it's important to remember that birds prefer a choice of levels for eating and building their nests. Having a slightly open spot with feeding trays close to ground level will satisfy the eating habits of birds that don't like hanging feeders, including mourning doves, thrashers, sparrows, cardinals, towhees, and dark-eyed juncos.

If you do spread seed directly on the ground, the site should be well-drained, and you should rake up excess food weekly and compost it, especially when it has been dampened by rain. To provide protection, the plants should be low-growing. Try ground feeding next to a low stone wall planted with a groundcover such as periwinkle (*Vinca minor*) or some of the slower-growing ivy cultivars. Or choose a small area surrounded by ferns for ground feeding.

Another great way to attract birds to the backyard garden is to plant a flower border of annual and perennial flowers in front of a line of shrubs or small trees so they serve as a background to the plantings. A line of junipers (*Juniperus* spp.), Oregon grape holly (*Mahonia aquifolium*), or perhaps fragrant sumac (*Rhus aromatica*) will become, not only a great backdrop for flowers, but also a fine place for birds to hide while darting in and out of the garden, and a valuable source of food as well.

Robins are ground feeders. Here, an entire flock searches for dinner under a hawthorn. Watching the males stake out their territories is great springtime entertainment.

Plants for birds

There are hundreds of plants that are attractive to birds. On the next few pages, you'll find some of the best, along with the birds that they attract.

Evergreen trees

An especially good evergreen tree for a bird garden is the 40-foot western or Sierra juniper (*Juniperus occidentalis*), hardy to Zone 5. The bluish-black berry-like cones are a favorite food of grosbeaks and waxwings, and the needles make especially fine cover for robins, sparrows, and juncos. The eastern red cedar (*Juniperus virginiana*) and the western red cedar or Rocky Mountain juniper (*J. scopulorum*) reach a height of 40 feet, and their berry-like cones provide both food and cover for many birds, including jays and waxwings. Both are hardy to Zone 3. Junipers also provide nesting sites for robins, sparrows, mockingbirds, and others.

Other evergreens that are valuable for shielding birds from harsh winters are Canadian hemlock (*Tsuga canadensis*), hardy to Zone 3, and Carolina hemlock (*T. caroliniana*), hardy to Zone 5. Warblers, robins, juncos, goldfinches, and bluejays like to nest in hemlocks. Douglas fir (*Pseudotsuga menziesii*), hardy to Zone 3, and other firs offer shelter to robins, blue jays, tanagers, and grosbeaks, while spruces such as the Colorado spruce (*Picea pungens*) are favored by warblers and sparrows. Eastern white pine (*Pinus strobus*), hardy to Zone 3, and other pines provide shelter and nesting places for robins, purple and house finches, mourning doves, and other birds. Most of these conifers are available in cultivars that mature at 12 feet tall; choose these if your yard is small.

Deciduous trees

Deciduous trees lose their leaves over the winter, but they still can provide food and shelter for birds. The following species are especially valuable in the wildlife garden.

The thick branching of black haw (*Viburnum prunifolium*), hardy to

Berries of trees and shrubs are an important food source for many birds. This female eastern bluebird is dining on a holly berry.

Zone 3, provides cover, and in late summer and fall its berries are eaten by many birds and other creatures. Most viburnums are shrubs, but this species grows as a small tree or a shrub, to about 12 feet tall. Flowering dogwoods (*Cornus florida*) can reach a height of 30 feet and are hardy to Zone 5. They're lovely when they bloom in the spring, and the trees are covered with red berries in the fall that many animals covet. Hawthorns (*Crataegus* spp.), including scarlet-fruited cockspur hawthorn (*C. crus-galli*), hardy to Zone 4, are favorite nesting spots for cardinals, buntings, wood thrushes, hummingbirds, and, in the Southwest, roadrunners. Their small red fruits are sought out by waxwings and thrushes.

Another good choice is crabapple (*Malus* spp.). There are many different species and cultivars that grow less than 30 feet tall. Most are hardy to Zone 4, but check before you buy. In spring, the trees are covered with showy white, pink, or rose blossoms. The small applelike fruits are eaten by finches, pheasants, and waxwings in fall, and when they fall to the ground, by deer, rabbits, foxes, and smaller mammals. Oak trees (*Quercus* spp.) are popular nesting sites for blue jays, orchard orioles, blue-gray gnatcatchers, and other birds. Alders (*Alnus* spp.) and mulberries (*Morus* spp.) provide shelter for many species.

Besides food sources, birds need trees and shrubs for cover and nesting sites. This yellow-throated vireo has hung its nest from a branch.

Shrubs

Several shrubs that are good choices for wildlife gardens are discussed in "Woodland trees and shrubs" on page 47. In addition, the following low shrubs provide both cover and food for birds. Blueberries (*Vaccinium* spp.) and blackberries (*Rubus* spp.) are devoured by over 100 species of birds, and other small—and larger—creatures feed on them, too. Small birds such as sparrows and common yellowthroats build nests among the bushes and brambles. Bayberries and wax myrtles (*Myrica* spp.) reach a height of about 9 feet (wax myrtle is a bit taller). Their white, berry-like fruits are eaten by warblers, catbirds, and swallows. Hardiness for all these plants varies with the species; check to see which ones are appropriate for your area. The red fruit of the common spicebush (*Lindera benzoin*), hardy to Zone 5, is a favorite food of thrushes. And gooseberry and currant bushes (*Ribes* spp.), both hardy to Zone 3, produce dark red to black berries that are eaten by magpies, catbirds, robins, and even white-tailed deer.

Also look for the American elder or common elder (*Sambucus canadensis*), hardy to Zone 3, which bears flat clusters of small black berries that are eaten by over 30 species of birds. Native roses (*Rosa* spp.) provide nesting sites for cardinals, towhees, sparrows, indigo

A pair of evening grosbeaks eat hawthorn berries. In addition to shrubs, you can also plant vines such as Virginia creeper (*Parthenocissus quinquefolia*) to make food for birds.

buntings, and other small birds. Many birds like to dine on the vitamin C-rich fruits (called hips) that form in summer or fall. Many songbirds love the white fruits of red-osier dogwood (*Cornus sericea*), and the plant's coral-red stems add a bright shot of color to the winter landscape. It's hardy to Zone 3. Another good choice is the American cranberry bush viburnum or highbush cranberry (*Viburnum trilobum*), hardy to Zone 2, which supplies both bright scarlet berries and cover. Finally, consider including scarlet firethorn (*Pyracantha coccinea*), hardy to Zone 5, in your bird landscape. Waxwings, mockingbirds, and robins relish its orange berries.

Native grasses

Dozens of native grasses are attractive enough to be ornamental, and their flower heads provide a wide variety of seeds. Broomsedge bluestem (*Andropogon virginicus*), June grass (*Koeleria cristata*), northern sea oats (*Chasmanthium latifolium*), Indian grass (*Sorghastrum nutans*), buffalo grass (*Buchloë dactyloides*), and switchgrass (*Panicum virgatum*) are all good candidates for the wildlife garden. In fact, most ornamental grasses make great bird-attracting plants since their handsome seedheads provide food from late summer into winter.

Indian grass (*Sorghastrum nutans*) is a good source of seeds for birds in prairie gardens.

Special features

In Chapter Three, we mentioned that a minimum of cleanup is needed in the wildlife garden. Some pruning might be necessary, especially when dead limbs or trunks could pose a danger to the garden's owners. But basically, the most successful bird gardeners try to make their gardens look a little messy. That's because these canny gardeners know that features like brush piles and vines attract the most birds to their yards. Here are some of their secrets.

Make a bower

A bower is a tangle of vines and branches that serves as shelter for birds and other wildlife. But instead of being completely wild and often choking the upper reaches of trees and bushes, the vines of a bower are under the gardener's control. Bowers provide excellent cover—and often food as well—for many kinds of birds, and bring a romantic, untamed look to a corner of the garden. If you grow a beautiful trumpet vine (*Campsis radicans*) or honeysuckle (*Lonicera* spp.), you may be lucky enough to attract hummingbirds to your bower. English ivy (*Hedera helix*) provides year-round cover, and Boston ivy (*Parthenocissus tricuspidata*) and Virginia creeper (*P. quinquefolia*) have brilliant red fall cover. Porcelain ampelopsis (*Ampelopsis brevipedunculata*) offers colorful autumn berries of stunning metallic turquoise that birds love.

By making tripods with bamboo or plastic stakes, and then training annual or perennial vines to grow on them, you can create marvelous bird shelters as well as focal points for your garden. To make a tripod, fasten three 6- to 8-foot poles together at the top, and anchor the bottoms 6 to 12 inches deep in the soil. Morning glories (*Ipomoea* spp.), hop vines (*Humulus* spp.), Virginia creeper, and even American bittersweet (*Celastrus scandens*) will readily twine around and clamber up the stakes to make perfect bowers for all kinds of birds. Virginia creeper and American bittersweet also produce small berries that are attractive to mockingbirds, sapsuckers, and flickers, while a number of mammals use them for winter foraging.

Seed sources for birds

These plants are good sources of seeds. Leave the flowers on when they fade so seeds will form.

Black-eyed Susan (*Rudbeckia hirta*), 1–3 feet tall. Coarse, oblong leaves; golden daisy-like flowers with stiff, dark brown centers, from midsummer into fall. Short-lived perennial grown as self-sowing annual.

Corn poppy (*Papaver rhoeas*), to 3 feet tall. Narrow leaves are hairy and divided into segments; 2-inch bright red, scarlet, purple, or white flowers in summer on wiry stems. Annual.

Forget-me-nots (*Myosotis* spp.), 1–1½ feet tall when in bloom; leaves grow close to the ground. Small woodland plants with soft oval leaves; branched clusters of small sky blue flowers with yellow centers. The annual species blooms in spring, perennial flowers from spring into early summer. Both types self-sow and spread. Perennial is hardy in Zones 4–8.

Iceland poppy (*Papaver nudicaule*), 1–2 feet tall. Basal cluster of light green leaves with fringed and cut edges; crepe-paper-like, broad-petaled flowers in shades of red, orange, pink, yellow, and white, with yellow centers, on wiry stems. Short-lived perennial often grown as annual. Zones 4–8.

Oriental poppy (*Papaver orientale*), 2–4 feet tall. Bristly, hairy leaves, deeply toothed or lobed, die-back after plants bloom; large summer flowers in brilliant red and orange, also shades of pink, salmon, and white, with dark centers, on tall stems. Zones 3–9.

Purple coneflower (*Echinacea purpurea*) 3–4 feet tall. Oval leaves; long-lasting, purple-pink daisy-like flowers with orange to brown centers in late summer. Zones 3–10.

Snapdragon (*Antirrhinum majus*), 6 inches–3 feet tall. Narrow elliptical leaves; stiff spikes of two-lipped, beak-shaped flowers in shades of red, pink, orange, yellow, and white in summer. Plants may rebloom in fall if cut back after first blooming; wait until birds eat the seeds. Annual.

Sunflowers (*Helianthus* spp.), 3–12 feet tall, depending on the species (below). Annual or perennial plants with large, coarsely toothed leaves; large, daisy-like summer flowers in golden yellow, with large brown, purple, or yellow centers. Most perennial species are hardy from Zones 3–10.

The red-bellied woodpecker enjoys visiting feeders. As you can see, this woodpecker actually has a gray-white belly; the red is on the top and back of its head.

Create areas of leaf litter

While not appealing to every bird that might visit your garden, small areas covered with a thick leaf mulch are a magnet for thrashers, towhees, and some sparrows. They will jump into the mulch, then do a modified "moon walk" as they scratch and hop around looking for bits of food. Many birds also use leaf skeletons in nest construction.

Brush piles for nests

In Chapter One we discussed brush piles as one of the most important wildlife lures you can construct. At the edge of a pond or stream, such piles become nesting spots for waterfowl; in a woodland environment, brush piles will do the same for land birds such as wrens.

Don't deadhead all the flowers

Gardeners have been told over the years about the importance of dead-heading (removing spent flowers) to force many plants to continue producing flowers. But deadheading prevents the formation of seeds. So in the wildlife garden, it's important to let some of the flowers mature in order to produce seeds for food. Purple coneflower (*Echinacea purpurea*), black-eyed Susans (*Rudbeckia* spp.), sunflowers (*Helianthus* spp.), and roses (*Rosa* spp.) are especially good food sources for birds. Snapdragons (*Antirrhinum majus*), poppies (*Papaver* spp.), and forget-me-nots (*Myosotis* spp.) are other good choices.

Supplemental feeding

No matter how extensive our wildlife gardens are, there's always room for more food—especially for birds. And birds are a lot like people when it comes to eating: A little variety is always welcome. Most of the year there is enough natural food available, but when you create a wildlife garden, you lay out the welcome mat. So when fall comes around, it's time to increase the quantity and variety of supplemental foods that you provide. It's a smart idea to include a line item for bird food when planning a family food budget. That way you'll never forget to provide for their needs as well.

Don't overfill feeders or put in more seed than the birds are likely to eat in a day.

How much seed do you need?

Never fill feeders with more seed than they can comfortably hold, and never put more seed on the ground than will be easily eaten in a day. Rotting or mildewed seeds and other foods can make a bird ill and spread disease. With animals as with humans, cleanliness has its virtues. And uneaten seed left on the ground can attract other hungry visitors, like rodents, that may be less welcome.

All-season feeding

The winter has passed, spring is rushing in with flowering trees and wildflowers, and pleasant weather is now the rule rather than the exception. So you ask yourself, "Should we continue to feed the birds?"

The answer is, "It all depends." At some point, it simply won't be necessary anymore. In most of the country, you will probably be able to stop feeding in May; in the Deep South, most migrant seed eaters will have left by mid-March. But if you miss the colorful company at the feeder, it's perfectly all right to continue to feed throughout the year. And remember—birds need a source of water all year, not just in winter or summer.

Feeding in summer will draw a more diverse assortment of birds to your garden, and will probably encourage more of them to nest and raise young in the area as well.

Blue jays are among the most entertaining feeder birds, but a group of jays can quickly empty a feeder.

Changing the diet

With the arrival of summer heat, it's a good idea to stop serving up foods like suet and peanut butter that have a high fat content (the fat goes rancid quickly in hot weather). And standard seed mixes with a high percentage of proso millet and some cracked corn may primarily attract birds such as common grackles, cowbirds, and European starlings, that you do not want.

Instead, you should rely on sunflower seed, niger seed, and/or a good-quality wild bird seed mix. Sunflower seeds are always a good choice—they will attract many seed eaters along with their young. Chickadees and titmice are especially entertaining to watch as the youngsters learn the ropes, and they always flock to tube feeders stocked with sunflower seed.

Citrus fruits, as well as bananas, apples, and raisins, will attract orioles, grosbeaks, catbirds, thrushes, and tanagers in many parts of the country. Even woodpeckers that normally live on a diet of insects sometimes take fruit. In fact, many seed eaters will eat fruit and other foods as well. Cut oranges and apples into slices or halves before putting them out; peel bananas and cut them in chunks. You can even buy special fruit feeders to hang from your trees.

Other foods for birds

Some birds will be attracted by sweet liquids served in a special dispenser. A solution of 4 parts water and 1 part table sugar, placed in small plastic vials and then wired to shrubs and trees, is also a popular treat and will draw hummingbirds and a number of other birds as well. Mixing water and grape juice may attract treetop dwellers like orioles (the Baltimore or northern oriole in the East and Bullock's and other species in the West and Southwest), especially if you have large trees in or next to your yard. It's fine to use red plastic feeders, but don't dye the sugar water red; red dye could be harmful to birds. See "Supplemental feeders" on page 122 for more on hummingbird feeders.

Tube feeders are perfect for small birds like goldfinches, house finches, and pine siskins.

A black-capped chickadee pecks a meal of thistle seed from a small hole in this feeder.

Water for birds

It's important to remember that birds dislike dirty birdbaths as much as people dislike a ring around the tub. Make sure all your birdbaths (and small pools) are clean of droppings and of algae and bacteria. You will probably need to scrub out birdbaths and replace the water every couple of days.

Songbirds are greatly attracted to moving water. Hang a trickle tube or small hose over a birdbath so that the water falls drop by drop—an important signal to remind local birds that water is available.

Even though birdbaths on pedestals are attractive in the wildlife garden, it's a good idea to place a second birdbath basin directly on the ground. Then place some clean rocks on the bottom so that birds will have a place to perch while bathing. When buying such containers, look for shallow basins with gently sloping, textured sides.

Birds all act differently in a birdbath. Some take quick, dainty dips while others, like this chickadee, hop right in and flutter their wings to give themselves a good dousing.

Dusting

Some birds prefer (or require) dust as a cleansing agent for their feathers. House sparrows, ring-necked pheasants, and quail of all sorts will scratch around in dusty soil. Then using the same movements as they do when bathing, they toss the dust around. Apparently such actions help the birds control small parasites that can hide among the many parts of a feather.

Nesting boxes and feeders

Housing cats and dogs can be an expensive proposition, but when it comes to birdhouses (or, as they are known today, nesting boxes) and feeders, dozens of different designs are now on the market, most of them very reasonably priced. As with most things in life, simplicity is best, especially when it comes to upkeep. The bird doesn't care if there is a thatched roof on his or her house, but once that thatch starts to deteriorate, you might lose interest in keeping up the rest of the house and it is the birds who suffer.

Building simple birdhouses

It is relatively easy to build a birdhouse (or nesting box). Choose cypress, recycled redwood, or other weather-resistant wood. The design should call for the house interior to be warm and dry, which means a pitched roof with some overhang. Just to be sure that there is no way for water to collect, drill a few small holes in the birdhouse floor. And either the roof, a side, or the bottom should be hinged to allow for easy cleaning at the end of the season.

Types of feeders

When it comes to buying feeders, look for designs that are reasonably easy to clean. The clear plastic tubular feeders are especially good because they cater to a number of birds. With all feeders, you will have to contend with hungry squirrels, eager to get at whatever you've set out for the birds. Tubular feeders can be installed with protective baffles to keep the pesky creatures at bay. You can purchase a smooth plastic dome to suspend above the feeder (on the same hanger) as a baffle to exclude squirrels, or use old long-playing phonograph records for the same purpose.

Another way to thwart squirrels is a pole-mounted feeder, especially if you put baffles above and below, making sure the pole is far enough away from nearby branches to prevent squirrels from leaping over (and they do leap!). Coating the pole with grease, Teflon, or Tanglefoot will

Nesting boxes built to specific dimensions are helping build bluebird populations in the eastern United States. The entry hole must also be the right size and at the right height to appeal to bluebirds.

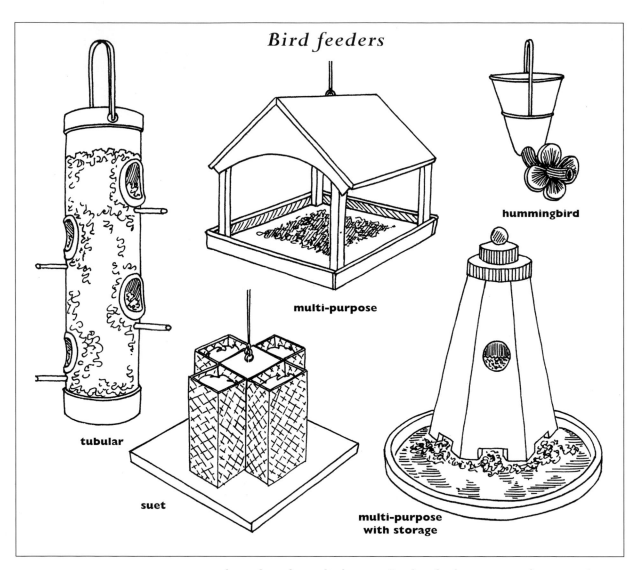

Bird feeders

tubular

multi-purpose

hummingbird

suet

multi-purpose
with storage

keep them from climbing it. Costlier feeders come with springs that will close feed openings under the weight of squirrels but stay open for less hefty wildlife such as birds.

Other bird feeder choices include a flat tray with squared-off compartments and a pitched roof to keep the food dry; suet feeders made of wire; or even a coconut with a section removed. Some tubular feeders have been modified to include smaller feeding ports and are perfect for the niger thistle seed that goldfinches and siskins love.

Nest box dimensions

SPECIES	BOX DEPTH (inches)	BOX HEIGHT (inches)	ENTRANCE HEIGHT (inches)	ENTRANCE DEPTH (inches)	PLACEMENT HEIGHT (feet)
American robin*	6 x 8	8	—	—	6–15
Barn swallow*	6 x 6	6	—	—	8–12
Chickadee	4 x 4	8–10	6–8	1⅛	6–15
Eastern and western bluebird	5 x 5	8–12	6–10	1½	5
Northern flicker	7 x 7	16–18	14–16	2½	6–20
Flycatcher, ash-throated	6 x 6	8–12	6–10	1½	5–15
Flycatcher, great crested	6 x 6	8–12	6–10	1¾	5–15
Nuthatch, brown-headed pygmy and red-breasted	4 x 4	8–10	6–8	1¼	5–15
Nuthatch, white-breasted	4 x 4	8–10	6–8	1⅜	12–20
Owl, barn	10 x 18	15–18	4	6	12–18
Owl, screech	8 x 8	12–15	9–12	3	10–30
Phoebe*	6 x 6	6	—	—	8–12
Prothonotary warbler	5 x 5	6	4–5	1⅛	4–8
Purple martin	6 x 6	6	1–2	2½	10–20
Titmouse	4 x 4	10–12	6–10	1¼	6–15
Woodpecker, downy	4 x 4	8–10	6–8	1¼	5–15
Woodpecker, hairy	6 x 6	12–15	9–12	1½	12–20
Woodpecker, red-headed	6 x 6	12–15	9–12	2	10–20
Wren, house or Bewick's	4 x 4	6–8	4–6	1¼	5–10
Wren, Carolina	4 x 4	6–8	4–6	1½	6–10
Yellow-bellied sapsucker	5 x 5	12–15	9–12	1½	10–20

*Use nesting shelf platform with three sides and an open front.

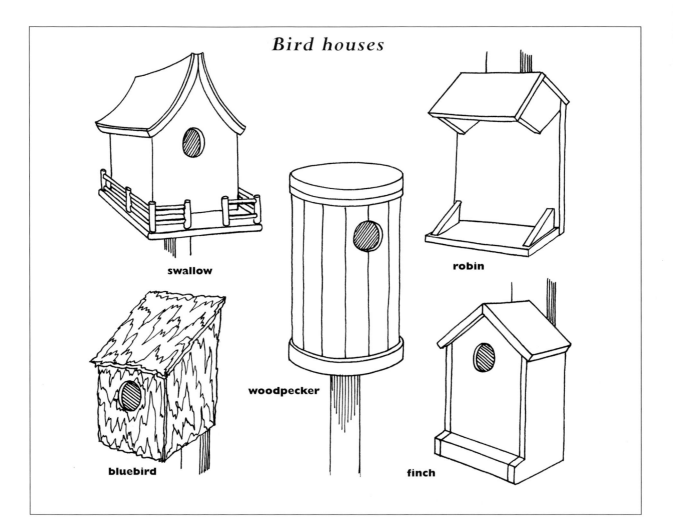

Bird houses

swallow

bluebird

woodpecker

robin

finch

✑ Building feeding stations

You can also make perfectly good feeders on your own. Create feeders from plastic milk jugs, bleach bottles, or pop bottles by cutting two feeding ports (about 3 inches square) about 2 inches up from the bottle's base. These ports allow birds to fly in for food. Put small drainage holes in the bottom and hang the feeder from a wire stuck through two holes in the bottle's neck. While not as beautiful as a redwood feeder, it's just as efficient. You can also easily make a feeding table with an open shallow tray, box, or board that can be set on a post or tree trunk 1 to 1½ feet off the ground. Some birds are uncomfortable at or unable to cling to hanging feeders but will readily visit trays. Among those preferring more open feeders installed closer to the ground are juncos, jays, cardinals, sparrows, and doves.

Preferred feeder habitats

It's great to have a feeder or two near a window so that you can watch the birds up close. (Feeders can be made or bought with suction cups or bracket attachments that allow them to sit on a windowsill or attach directly to the glass.) But you should place other feeders—with a variety of feeds—away from the house and in the wilder part of the garden. Tree branches, shrubbery, or thickets are great locations, especially since they provide plenty of cover from cats and other predators. And in the winter, make sure you locate a feeder or two away from winter winds so birds have protection from the weather, too.

Cleaning them out

Once a year, usually in the fall, it is important to give your feeders and birdhouses a thorough cleaning. By then, birds will have finished their nesting and the houses will not be needed again until next spring. Old nest materials harbor parasites that may attack the young of next year's brood. Removing everything in the nest box assures healthier young in the spring. For birds like bluebirds who nest two or more times a year, don't wait for fall to clean up. Instead, clean out nest boxes when the fledglings have left the nest.

It is also a good idea to clean bird feeders regularly when they are in use. Once a month, scrub feeders with a mild detergent combined with a solution of 1 part chlorine bleach to 10 parts water. Rinse thoroughly with clear water, and let dry completely before refilling the feeders with fresh seed. And remember to clean up the seed hulls and droppings that collect under feeders on a regular basis. Ground-feeding birds could become ill if they ingest old spoiled hulls or spilled seeds tainted with droppings.

Don't be too quick to remove dead trees from your property, as long as they are not in danger of falling. They provide ideal nesting sites for cavity nesters like this red-headed woodpecker.

Hummingbirds

A ruby-throated hummingbird sips nectar from the tubular flowers of trumpet creeper (*Campsis radicans*).

A sugar-water feeder that features a little red on it will attract and nourish hummingbirds.

Everybody loves hummingbirds. They are probably the most popular birds, and we all want to bring them to our wildlife gardens. The blur of their fast-beating wings in combination with their iridescent colors—which are not from pigments but from their prism-like feathers—always makes for a terrific show.

Plants to attract hummers

Hummingbirds love wildflowers. They are especially attracted to cardinal flower (*Lobelia cardinalis*), bee balm (*Monarda didyma*), trumpet creeper (*Campsis radicans*), wild columbine (*Aquilegia canadensis*), scarlet bugler (*Penstemon centranthifolius*), and crimson columbine (*Aquilegia formosa*). They will also visit four-o'clock (*Mirabilis jalapa*), red salvias (*Salvia* spp.), aloes (*Aloe* spp.), certain azaleas (*Rhododendron* spp.), morning glories (*Ipomoea* spp.), trumpet honeysuckle (*Lonicera sempervirens*), and even hosta flowers (*Hosta* spp.).

If hummers are your favorite birds, consider creating a special garden just for them. Plant a selection of their favorite flowers, then sit back and enjoy both the lovely flowers and their comical little visitors.

Supplemental feeders

For hummingbirds, choose a bright red plastic feeder because these tiny birds are especially attracted to that color. If you can only find a clear feeder, tie a big red bow to the top. Hang the feeder in the shade where you can easily see it, but don't put it too close to a window. Otherwise, hummingbirds might fly at their own reflected image and be injured.

To feed hummingbirds, mix a solution of 4 parts water and 1 part table sugar, heating it only enough to dissolve the sugar. Do not make the solution any stronger because higher concentrations of sugar may ultimately cause kidney or liver damage to these birds. Feeders should be cleaned out every three days so that the sugar does not ferment, which might harm visiting birds.

Hummingbird flowers

Aloes (*Aloe* spp.). Plant size varies with species. Green or blue-green foliage in rosettes; tubular red or yellow flowers. Tender, succulent plants for frost-free gardens in the Southwest. Zone 10.

Bee balm (*Monarda didyma*), 2–4 feet tall. Oval leaves with toothed edges, aromatic when crushed; clusters of tubular flowers in 4-inch heads, in red, rosy pink, purple, or white, all summer. Full sun to light shade. Zones 4–8.

Cardinal flower (*Lobelia cardinalis*), 2–4 feet tall. Oblong to lance-shaped leaves; spikes of brilliant red flowers in mid- to late summer. Needs a moist location, prefers shade but tolerates full sun. Zones 2–9.

Crimson columbine (*Aquilegia formosa*), 2–4 feet tall. Red-and-yellow flowers from late spring to late summer. Native to western parts of North America. Zones 3–7.

Daylilies (*Hemerocallis fulva, H.* x *hybrida*), to 5 feet tall. Leaves are long, strap-shaped; clusters of large, trumpet-shaped flowers on tall, straight stems in summer. Blossoms of *H. fulva*, common daylily, are orange; flowers of *H.* x *hybrida* come in many shades of red, orange, pink, and yellow. Zones 3–9.

Fire pink (*Silene virginica*), to 2 feet tall. Clusters of red flowers in spring and summer; petals have toothed edges. Zones 3–9.

Four-o'clock (*Mirabilis jalapa*), to 3 feet tall. Funnel-shaped flowers are red, yellow or white, and open in late afternoon. Tender perennial grown as an annual north of Zone 10.

Jewelweed (*Impatiens capensis*), to 3 feet or taller. Bushy wildflower with oval leaves; small orange flowers all summer into fall. Does best in a moist, shady location. Zones 3–8.

Scarlet bugler (*Penstemon centranthifolius*), 2–3 feet tall. Narrow leaves; red flowers in early summer. Needs full sun and well-drained soil. Zones 3–10.

Scarlet sage (*Salvia splendens*), to 3 feet tall or taller. Dark green leaves; upright spikes of tiny flowers with brilliant scarlet bracts (that look like petals) throughout summer until frost. Perennial usually grown as an annual. Zones 4–7.

Texas sage (*Salvia coccinea*), to 2 feet tall, taller in warm climates. Spikes of scarlet flowers in spring and summer. Full sun. Tender perennial that grows big in warm climates; grown as an annual north of Zone 8.

Trumpet creeper (*Campsis radicans*). Woody deciduous vine to 40 feet long. Oval leaves; showy clusters of tubular, trumpet-shaped orange flowers during much of the summer. Best in full sun, but also tolerates partial to light shade. Zones 4–9.

Trumpet honeysuckle (*Lonicera sempervirens*). Woody deciduous vine, 10–15 feet long. Elliptical leaves; tubular scarlet, orange, or yellow flowers in summer. Native to the eastern U.S. Zones 3–9.

Wild columbine (*Aquilegia canadensis*), 1–3 feet tall. Compound lobed leaves in low clusters; yellow flowers with tubular spurs in late spring to early summer, carried on slender stems. Well-drained soil. Partial shade to full sun. Zones 3–8.

Chapter Seven

Gardening for Butterflies

Butterflies excite the imagination like no other living creatures. People who hate every insect they see and cringe at the sight of an ant or even a caterpillar are delighted when a butterfly crosses their path. For centuries, poets have written about butterflies, songs have been dedicated to their lilting flight, fanciers have collected them, and their splendid wings have been used or depicted in innumerable arts and crafts. Even the butterfly's common name has a pleasant derivation. It comes from the resemblance between the wing color of the common sulfur butterfly and freshly churned butter.

All about butterflies

Butterfly experts are called lepidopterists, a term taken from Lepidoptera, the insect order of butterflies and moths that includes over 11,000 species in North America alone. About 700 are butterflies; the rest are moths (see Chapter Eight). The word comes from the Greek words *lepis*, for scale, and *pteron*, for wing, and refers to the pigmented wing structure of these remarkable insects. The orders are further divided into many superfamilies, but for butterfly enthusiasts and gardeners there are only two you need to be familiar with. One is the true butterfly family (Papilionidae), a group of insects with slim bodies and large wings. The other is the skipper family (Hesperiidae), a group of insects with generally smaller, more triangular wings—in flight, it resembles the shape of the stealth bomber—and a thicker body.

Each autumn, monarchs from all over the country embark on a long migration to warm overwintering grounds in Mexico. Here, an adult monarch butterfly visits a bull thistle flower in a Missouri meadow.

Butterfly wings

The magnificent color of butterfly wings does not come from pigmentation directly on the wing, but from tiny scales that hang on the wing much like shingles on a house roof. These scales are so small they look like powder when rubbed onto the fingers.

There are two kinds of color in the butterfly's wing: pigmented and structural. The former includes the white of the wings and all of the beautiful yellows and oranges—which are derived from a butterfly waste product, urea—as well as the browns, blacks, and reds, which are also produced by the body's chemicals.

But many of the most beautiful colors in the wings are structural, and they are produced in the same way that colors are produced by a glass prism when it is struck by a ray of light or the sun. Fine parallel grooves like those on a phonograph record are set in particular patterns on the individual scales of the wing. The metallic or pearly streaks, the lovely blues, the coppers and the greens are all an effect of light striking these grooves. With the pigmented and structural colors often overlapping, the results are indeed striking and beautiful.

The butterfly life cycle

Probably no other insect's life cycle has been as widely represented in lore or legend as that of the butterfly. Many insects go through the stages of metamorphosis, but few wind up with the beauty of the butterfly.

The butterfly egg is the beginning of the cycle. The shapes of eggs vary greatly, ranging from tall and thin to turban-shaped to round or flat. Usually, related species of butterflies have similar egg shapes. With most species, the surface of the egg is ornamented with various grooves, knobs, or pits; others, however, are perfectly smooth.

The eggs hatch into tiny caterpillars, usually about $\frac{1}{100}$ inch long. The body of the caterpillar is segmented into distinct sections. Each of the three segments directly behind the head has a pair of short legs that end in a claw, and the next four have short false legs called prolegs that

Butterflies lay their eggs on or near host plants on which the caterpillars can feed. This monarch caterpillar rests on a leaf of the common milkweed, a favorite food.

end in tiny hooks (they help the caterpillar hold onto virtually any plant surface). The last segment has a pair of claspers, which the caterpillar uses when molting its larval skin.

Caterpillars have developed an amazing variety of special adaptations to help them survive. For protection, some have stinging spines or bristles; others give off noxious odors when disturbed; and some depend on camouflage or even have spots that look like huge eyes. Still others are poisonous to eat or have a bitter taste that their potential predators have learned to avoid.

Caterpillars grow by continually eating and expanding their bodies, then molting or shedding their previous skin to emerge in a larger form. But when larval growth is finally over, a strange change takes place. At that time, caterpillars turn into mummy-like creatures, called pupae or chrysalides, enshrouded in pupal cases. (Cocoons are simply silken covers around the pupae of certain moth species.) The pupal cases are often decorated with glistening knobs, intricate filagrees, or bright colors, and each species has a distinctive pattern.

After a period of time—which can vary, according to the species and the time of year, from about a week to more than a year—the pupal case or chrysalis splits and the butterfly crawls out, releases fluid into its wings to expand them, then dries them and flutters away.

Butterfly behavior

Just as some people walk quickly and others plod along, butterflies show striking variations in flight. Skippers quickly dart from place to place, swallowtails flutter, and monarchs glide along, seemingly without a worry in the world. Each species or group of species shows a characteristic flight pattern and, like many birds, can be as easily recognized by this behavior as by its color or size.

Many people know about the migratory flights of the monarchs, which make their way to Mexico and California in autumn. But other species of butterflies also follow less spectacular, and less understood, migratory patterns. The buckeye, the common sulphur, the mourning cloak, and the painted lady all give evidence of moving in groups from place to place.

We mentioned in Chapter Five the phenomenon of puddling, in which congregations of butterflies gather around puddles or patches of damp ground. Tiger and zebra swallowtails, buckeyes, blues, sulfur butterflies, and most skippers seem to have a particular fondness for group get-togethers at puddles that, at the risk of anthropomorphizing, look as much like social meetings as anything else.

When it comes to the study of butterfly behavior, the wildlife gardener can do a great deal for lepidopterists by taking careful notes on the activities of these insects. Many observations that have led to major scientific discoveries have been made by gifted amateurs working in their own backyards.

This group of blue butterflies is puddling. These gatherings of butterflies around puddles and wet spots look for all the world like meetings of friends or business associates. In reality, they are sipping water and minerals from the damp ground.

Attracting butterflies

Most butterflies are creatures of the open air and sunshine, rarely flying about on cloudy or rainy days. Some, however, seek the shadier parts of the garden. They might sit for a moment in a shaft of sunlight, but soon move to the shadows. Others spend their lives in the woods; unless there is a climatic disturbance like a hurricane or a natural disaster like a forest fire, you will probably never see these species in your garden. And don't bother to look for butterflies at night, for that time is especially reserved for the moths (although a few moths like the hummingbird, clearwing, and sphinx moths will fly by day). So if you are planning a butterfly garden, there are some key elements you can include that will maximize your garden's appeal and increase the number of your butterfly visitors.

Butterfly weed (*Asclepias tuberosa*) is one of the best plants to attract butterflies, such as this fritillary, to the garden. Butterfly weed is a close relative of milkweed, which is also a good butterfly plant.

A butterfly meadow

The meadow flowers listed in Chapter Four are surefire for attracting a large number of butterflies. Like magnets, all the native asters (*Aster* spp.)

draw butterflies, such as sulfurs, painted ladies, red admirals, and silver-spotted skippers. Giant skippers are partial to the flowers of yuccas (*Yucca* spp.), and swallowtails and many smaller species to blazing-stars (*Liatris* spp.) and Joe-Pye weed (*Eupatorium fistulosum*).

Scatter flowers throughout

If you want to have butterflies around your wildlife garden, be sure to grow flowers in as many places as possible. That means not only in the flower garden itself, but scattered all around the yard. The smaller milkweeds like butterfly weed (*Asclepias tuberosa*) are attractive selections for the more civilized parts of the garden. But in the wilder areas, you can grow common milkweed (*A. syriaca*) to provide food for monarch caterpillars as well as the caterpillars of swallowtails, cabbage whites, common sulfurs, many hairstreaks, question marks, common blues, great spangled fritillaries, mourning cloaks, painted ladies, red admirals, and dozens of species of skippers.

And remember to plant flowering vines. Honeysuckles are popular with many butterfly species. Trumpet honeysuckle (*Lonicera sempervirens*) is a safe choice that will not become rampant and invasive like some species of honeysuckle. Passionflowers (*Passiflora* spp.) are primary foods for both the larvae and adults of the gulf fritillary. And many of the plants that are at home in a rock garden are special favorites of butterflies. Many of the small garden pinks (*Dianthus* spp.) have strong, sweet fragrances that are loved by butterflies, especially swallowtails. Rock cresses (*Arabis* spp.) will attract the small but beautiful common blues. The lavenders (*Lavandula* spp.) are also butterfly favorites.

Food for caterpillars

The flower preferred by a butterfly is not necessarily the food of choice for its caterpillar. The leaves of most woodland grasses are special favorites of the caterpillars of the large wood nymph and the tawny-edged skipper, but are overlooked by butterflies because they offer no nectar.

Attracting butterflies in the shade garden

Most butterflies love the sun and will only feed in bright daylight. But if you have a shady lot, don't give up hope of attracting butterflies. Many woodland species, such as wood satyrs, wood nymphs, commas, and mourning cloaks can be encouraged to visit the woodland garden if you provide their favorite foods—overripe fruit and fermented tree sap.

Place rotting peaches or plums or a thick fruit pulp and sugar water concoction on shady logs and stumps. Butterflies will soon appear. These foods will also attract beautiful moths after dark.

If you have an oozing tree (usually caused by a heart rot fungus) on your property, keep it for the butterflies that will visit it. Although diseased, the tree will continue to live for years and will supply some of the food needs of many generations of butterflies.

The caterpillar of the lovely buckeye dotes on the leaves of the English plantain (*Plantago lanceolata*), a plant that is cursed by anyone with a lawn. These are just a few of the many cases where weeds that do not belong in the garden proper are a must for the wildlife garden. Other caterpillar choices include parsley (*Petroselinum crispum*), the number-one food plant of the eastern black swallowtail. (In fact, its caterpillar is known as the parsley worm.) Its western cousin, the anise swallowtail, enjoys parsley as well as fennel (*Foeniculum vulgare*) and members of the carrot family.

Shelter from strong winds

Like the beautiful large wood nymph, most large butterflies, while appreciating a gentle breeze to help them move along their flight path, seem to resent hard winds. Having flowers in a somewhat sheltered area, where the butterflies can alight to feed and move around without being blown about, is an added attraction of any butterfly garden.

The viceroy butterfly is a mimic: It looks like the monarch, which has a bad taste that protects it from predators. The look-alike viceroy fools potential predators into thinking it, too, is not good to eat.

Plants to attract butterflies

Most flowers are visited by many more insects than just bees and butterflies, but the flowers of the following plants are known especially to attract a large number of butterflies.

Shrubs

High on any list of shrubs to attract butterflies are the butterfly bushes (*Buddleia* spp.). Their highly fragrant flowers will attract swallowtails, commas, Milbert's tortoiseshells, monarchs, painted ladies, and red admirals. The silver-gray leaves, lavender flower spikes, and arching branches of fountain buddleia (*B. alternifolia*) give this 12-foot shrub a graceful appearance.

When in bloom, buttonbushes (*Cephalanthus* spp.) provide nectar for American painted ladies, monarchs, and tiger swallowtails. And in the West, gray rabbitbrush (*Chrysothamnus nauseosus*) attracts orange sulfurs and painted ladies. Other shrubs that attract butterflies are bluebeards (*Caryopteris* spp.), old-fashioned weigela (*Weigela florida*), species azaleas (*Rhododendron* spp.), and ceanothus (*Ceanothus* spp.).

A tiger swallowtail perches on a butterfly bush flower cluster. Butterfly bushes (*Buddleia* spp.) attract many kinds of butterflies. The plants are easy to grow in full sun. Their flowers come in shades of purple, pink, and white.

Perennials

Along with thistle flowers (*Cirsium* spp.), black-eyed Susans (*Rudbeckia fulgida*) are nectar sources for the great spangled fritillary and the pearly crescentspot. Queen Anne's lace (*Daucus carota* var. *carota*) not only feeds the caterpillars of the eastern black swallowtail but provides nectar for swallowtails and common hairstreaks. See "Food plants for butterflies and caterpillars" on page 138 for more plant suggestions.

Monarch butterflies are usually drawn to flowers in the Composite or Daisy Family, as well as butterfly bush and other milkweeds, but here a group seeks nectar from a native blue lobelia growing in Missouri.

Plants to support caterpillars

I f you doubt that butterflies have certain food preferences, consider the story of the European cabbage butterfly. It was accidentally introduced into Québec, Canada in the early 1860's. Some 130 years later, these small insects have become pests throughout the entire continent. When adults are ready to lay eggs, they look for almost any member of the cabbage (or mustard) family, and the resulting green caterpillars begin to do their damage. Vegetable gardeners know the preferences of these insects all too well—they prefer broccoli, cabbage, collards, and kale.

Other plants nourish the caterpillars of more desirable butterflies. For example, New England asters (*Aster novae-angliae*) supply food for caterpillars of the little pearly crescentspot, a species common from Canada to Mexico. Any females with eggs will be sure to stop if they see the plants. The caterpillars of the giant swallowtail have a fondness for citrus trees in the South, prickly ashes (*Zanthoxylum* spp.), hop tree (*Ptelea* spp.), and of all things, the gas plant (*Dictamnus albus*), an attractive plant for the perennial border. The caterpillars of black swallowtails are especially fond of parsley.

A butterfly garden must contain food sources for caterpillars as well as nectar sources for adult butterflies. The caterpillar of the eastern black swallowtail, shown here, likes dill, parsley, carrots, wild carrot or Queen Anne's lace, and other plants in the Carrot Family (Umbelliferae).

Butterflies before and after

The photographs on these two pages show five commonly seen butterflies in their larval and adult stages, with the larva of each butterfly on the left, and its adult counterpart on the right.

The delicate painted lady can be found across the U.S. and is particularly partial (in its butterfly incarnation) to wildflowers and butterfly bush, while the spicebush swallowtail limits itself to meadows and woodlands throughout the eastern U.S.

The tiger swallowtail also inhabits the eastern U.S., as well as the Canadian west coast north to Alaska. The giant swallowtail ranges as far west as the Rockies, feeding on goldenrod, lantana, and citrus trees. The familiar, richly colored monarch makes its home in a wide variety of habitats in every region of the U.S. except the very northwest corner.

Painted lady larva

Painted lady adult

Spicebush swallowtail larva

Spicebush swallowtail adult

Tiger swallowtail larva

Tiger swallowtail adult

Giant swallowtail larva

Giant swallowtail adult

Monarch larvae

Monarch adult

Food plants for butterflies and caterpillars

SPECIES	LARVAL FOOD	ADULT FOOD
Alfalfa butterfly (*C. eurytheme*)	Alfalfa (*Medicago* spp.), clovers (*Trifolium* spp.)	Clovers, thistles (*Cirsium* spp.), dogwoods (*Cornus* spp.)
American painted lady (*Vanessa virginiensis*)	Pearly everlastings (*Anaphalis* spp.), pussy-toes (*Antennaria* spp.), cudweeds (*Gnaphalium* spp.)	Common heliotrope (*Heliotropium arborescens*), yarrows (*Achillea* spp.), zinnia (*Zinnia elegans*), butterfly bushes (*Buddleia* spp.)
Banded hairstreak (*Satyrium calanus*)	Oaks (*Quercus* spp.), walnuts (*Juglans* spp.)	Milkweeds (*Asclepias* spp.), sumac (*Rhus* spp.), dogbanes (*Apocynum* spp.), sweet pepperbush (*Clethra alnifolia*)
Black swallowtail (*Papilio polyxenes*)	Dill (*Anethum graveolens*), Queen Anne's lace (*Daucus carota* var. *carota*), parsley (*Petroselinum crispum*), fennel (*Foeniculum vulgare*)	Milkweeds (*Asclepias* spp.), thistles (*Cirsium* spp.), phlox (*Phlox* spp.)
Buckeye (*Junonia coenia*)	Plantains (*Plantago* spp.), toadflax (*Linaria* spp.), snapdragon (*Antirrhinum majus*)	Many wildflowers
Cabbage white (*Pieris rapae*)	Mustard family members (Cruciferae), including cabbage, Brussels sprouts, kale, mustard, and collards	Mustard family members
Checkered skipper (*Pyrgus communis*)	Hollyhocks (*Alcea* spp.), velvetleaf (*Abutilon theophrasti*)	Fleabanes (*Erigeron* spp.), wild asters (*Aster* spp.), shepherd's needle (*Scandix pecten-veneris*), red clover (*Trifolium pratense*)
Checkered white (*Pieris protodice*)	Cabbage, turnip, mustard, sweet alyssum (*Lobularia maritima*)	Great variety of garden and wildflowers
Clouded sulphur (*Colias philodice*)	Medics (*Medicago* spp.), white clover (*Trifolium repens*), vetches (*Vicia* spp.)	Goldenrods (*Solidago* spp.), phlox (*Phlox* spp.), milkweeds (*Asclepias* spp.)
Common wood nymph (*Cercyonis pegala*)	Purple-top (*Tridens flavus*) and other native grasses	Overripe fruit, occasionally flowers
Coral hairstreak (*Satyrium titus*)	Wild cherries and plums (*Prunus* spp.)	Butterfly weed (*Asclepias tuberosa*), sweet pepper bush (*Clethra alnifolia*)
Eastern tailed blue (*Everes comyntas*)	Bush clovers (*Lespedeza* spp.), everlasting peas (*Lathyrus* spp.), white clover (*Trifolium repens*)	Many wild and garden flowers, especially those in the pea family
Giant swallowtail (*Papilio cresphontes*)	Prickly ashes (*Zanthoxylum* spp.), gas plant (*Dictamnus albus*), citrus (*Citrus* spp.)	Honeysuckles (*Lonicera* spp.), goldenrods (*Solidago* spp.), azaleas (*Rhododendron* spp.), lantanas (*Lantana* spp.)
Gray hairstreak (*Strymon melinus*)	Hawthorns (*Crataegus* spp.), beans (*Phaseolus* spp.) and other pea family plants	Many wildflowers and garden flowers
Great spangled fritillary (*Speyeria cybele*)	Violets (*Viola* spp.)	Thistle (*Cirsium* spp.), dogbanes (*Apocynum* spp.), and other wildflowers
Hop merchant (*Polygonia comma*)	Hops (*Humulus* spp.), nettles (*Urtica* spp.), elms (*Ulmus* spp.)	Tree sap, overripe fruit
Little copper (*Lycaena phlaeas*)	Sheep sorrel (*Rumex acetosella*)	Yarrows (*Achillea* spp.)
Little wood satyr (*Megisto cymela*)	Various woodland grasses	Fermented tree sap, "aphid honeydew," white flowers

SPECIES	LARVAL FOOD	ADULT FOOD
Milbert's tortoiseshell (*Nymphalis milberti*)	Nettles (*Urtica* spp.)	Many wildflowers
Monarch (*Danaus plexippus*)	Milkweeds (*Asclepias* spp.)	Milkweeds, plus many wild and garden flowers
Mourning cloak (*Nymphalis antiopa*)	Elms (*Ulmus* spp.), willows (*Salix* spp.), hackberries (*Celtis* spp.)	Primarily tree sap (often at sapsucker drillings) and fermenting fruit
Northern cloudywing (*Thorybes pylades*)	Tick trefoil (*Desmodium* spp.), bush clovers, other legumes	Dogbanes (*Apocynum* spp.), white and pink milkweeds (*Asclepias* spp.), buttonbush (*Cephalanthus occidentalis*)
Olive hairstreak (*Mitoura grynea*)	Eastern red cedar (*Juniperus virginiana*)	Winter cress (*Barbarea vulgaris*), milkweeds (*Asclepias* spp.), dogbanes (*Apocynum* spp.)
Painted lady (*Vanessa cardui*)	Thistles (*Cirsium spp.*), hollyhocks (*Alcea* spp.), borage (*Borago officinalis*)	Many wildflowers, butterfly bushes (*Buddleia* spp.)
Pearly crescentspot (*Phyciodes tharos*)	Wild asters, including New England aster (*Aster novae-angliae*)	Asters, thistles (*Cirsium* spp.), milkweeds (*Asclepias* spp.)
Pipevine swallowtail (*Battus philenor*)	Birthwort (*Aristolochia* spp.)	Lilacs (*Syringa* spp.), milkweeds (*Asclepias* spp.), phlox (*Phlox* spp.)
Question mark (*Polygonia interrogationis*)	Elms (*Ulmus* spp.), hackberries (*Celtis* spp.), nettles (*Urtica* spp.)	Tree sap, overripe fruit
Red admiral (*Vanessa atalanta*)	Nettles (*Urtica* spp.), false nettles (*Boehmeria* spp.)	Tree sap and overripe fruit, milkweeds (*Asclepias* spp.), butterfly bushes (*Buddleia* spp.)
Roadside skipper (*Amblyscirtes vialis*)	Oats (*Avena* spp.), Kentucky bluegrass (*Poa pratensis*)	Ivies (*Hedera* spp.), self-heal (*Prunella vulgaris*)
Silver-spotted skipper (*Epargyreus clarus*)	Locusts (*Robinia* spp.), wisterias (*Wisteria* spp.), honey locust (*Gleditsia triacanthos*)	Many wild and garden flowers
Silvery checkerspot (*Charidryas nycteis*)	Sunflowers (*Helianthus* spp.), asters (*Aster* spp.), crown-beard (*Verbesina* spp.)	Sunflowers, coneflowers (*Echinacea* spp.)
Spring azure (*Celastrina ladon*)	Dogwoods (*Cornus* spp.), viburnums (*Viburnum* spp.)	Dogbanes (*Apocynum* spp.), milkweeds (*Asclepias* spp.), spicebush (*Lindera benzoin*), privets (*Ligustrum* spp.)
Tiger swallowtail (*Papilio glaucus*)	Tulip tree (*Liriodendron tulipifera*), ashes (*Fraxinus* spp.), wild cherries (*Prunus* spp.), birches (*Betula* spp.)	Bee balm (*Monarda didyma*), butterfly bushes (*Buddleia* spp.), clovers (*Trifolium* spp.), Mexican sunflowers (*Tithonia* spp.)
Variegated fritillary (*Euptoieta claudia*)	Passionflowers (*Passiflora* spp.), violets (*Viola* spp.)	Many wild and garden flowers
Viceroy (*Limenitis archippus*)	Willows (*Salix nigra* and *S. sericea*), aspens (*Populus* spp.)	Many tall daisy family wildflowers, carrion flowers (*Stapelia* spp.)
Western tiger swallowtail (*Papilio rutulus*)	Poplars (*Populus* spp.), willows	Butterfly bushes (*Buddleia* spp.) and many other garden wildflowers
Zebra swallowtail (*Eurytides marcellus*)	Pawpaws (*Asimina triloba*)	Milkweeds (*Asclepias* spp.) and many other wild and garden flowers

Chapter Eight

Gardening for Nightlife

Dusk—that magical time between day and night when colors blur, shapes seem to shift, and anything seems possible. At twilight, birds that have been silent since morning begin to sing. Wasps stop buzzing, dragonflies cease to fly, bumblebees and honeybees, finding it too late to head back to their nests, stop for the night in the protective shelter of a flower or hide under leaves. Fireflies flicker over lawns and fields. Bats silently circle above the trees, evening primroses open to the moon, and moths leave their daytime hideouts to fly out on the cool evening air.

The backyard at night

Sitting outside as dusk deepens to dark and the wildlife "night shift" comes on the job is an unforgettable experience. But all too often, even inveterate wildlife observers go inside when night takes over the backyard. This is perfectly understandable in the midst of a winter storm or summer downpour, but the same can't be said of other times. For nature never wastes time, and in the backyard, the wild garden, and out in the field and forest, there are as many things going on at night as there are during the day.

Who's active at night?

At night, insects abound outdoors: Fireflies flicker, moths flutter, and crickets sing to the moonlight. Small mammals hunt for food under cover of darkness. Bats use their natural radar to catch flying insects. Raccoons and opossums also search for food, often to the chagrin of suburb dwellers who find their garbage cans tipped over in the morning—or still occupied by a sated opussum. And above it all, the sharp-sighted nighthawks fly, and the owl listens for an unwary mouse.

Opossums are among the mammals that are most active at night. This one is having dinner at a suet feeder. Opossums are marsupials, like kangaroos, and carry their young in a pouch.

Night-flying moths

Like butterflies, moths are members of the order *Lepidoptera*, a group that includes over 11,000 species north of the Mexican border. Despite the great press that butterflies get, they account for only about 765 of these species; all the rest are moths.

Like the wings of butterflies, moth wings are covered with scales. Moths also share the same complex life cycle as butterflies, although most butterflies emerge from a structure called a chrysalis, while most moth caterpillars spin cocoons. And there are more significant differences between these two types of creatures. As with nocturnal mammals, moth eyes have a tapetum that enhances their vision at night. The male moth antennae are also usually far more complex than a butterfly's, and they react to the molecules of scent that female moths release. The antennae are also necessary to the moth's sense of balance—if they are removed, a moth cannot fly properly.

The lovely and mysterious-looking luna moth is large, with a 4-inch wingspan. It is drawn to night-blooming flowers.

Among the beautiful moths that are usually seen only at night are the pink-spotted hawkmoth; the exquisite sea-green luna moth, with a 4-inch wingspan measured from the tip of the showy forewings, and the largest North American moth, the cecropia, with 5- to 6-inch red-brown wings and beautiful brick, black, and white markings. Less attractive but far more common, the isabella tiger moth is familiar in its youth as the woolly bear caterpillar.

Tree frogs and toads

The nighttime chorus includes more than insects, for the frogs and toads have their own songs as well. The tiny spring peeper frogs are no more than 1¼ inches long, with brown skin and a large dark "X" on their backs. You usually hear these frogs trill in late afternoons and evenings toward the end of winter and beginning of spring. They lay eggs on plant stems growing in small ponds. Within seven weeks, the little frogs are ½ inch long and ready to leave the water. If you hear a frog "singing" from a tree (or the side of your house), it's probably the gray tree frog, which looks like lichen on the bark of a tree. Gray tree frogs are 1¼ to 2¼ inches long.

Larger commonly found frogs include the green frog, which is 2 to 4 inches long and ranges from Canada south to North Carolina and west to Oklahoma. The northern leopard frog, which is also called the meadow frog because it wanders far from water, can be found all across the northern United States and southern Canada. The southern leopard frog, usually measuring between 3 and 4 inches long, is a handsome frog with skin of green and brown. Both leopard frogs sport jaunty spots like their namesake. The bullfrog, with its throaty croak, may reach a whopping 8 inches long. The pig frog is also large—up to 6 inches—and prone to produce a gutteral grunt like a pig (a number of these frogs croaking together can sound like a herd of swine). The spotted frog, found in the Northwest and in Canada, is 2 to 4 inches long with warty-looking spots and legs with bright yellow undersides.

The green tree frog is quite small. It's nearly invisible as it perches in the foliage of a pine seedling.

Although some people are skittish about toads because of their warts, this is nothing but ill-grounded folklore. Toads don't cause warts in humans. Furthermore, they are valuable insect eaters and fascinating members of the backyard bestiary. The three most common toads in the East are the American toad, which grows up to 4 inches long and is brown and covered with glandular bumps; the Fowler's toad, usually about 3 inches long, with clearly defined brown markings on a whitish body, which appears in great numbers when heavy rains follow a long period of drought; and the eastern spadefoot, just over 2 inches long and brown with yellow lines running over the back. The West and South have, among other species, the western green toad at 1½ to 2 inches long, with its pale green skin and round black dots, and the western spadefoot, usually about 2 inches long and gray or brown with small dark markings. Spadefoot toads use their hind feet to dig burrows.

Owls, nighthawks, and other birds

Among the birds of the night, the most familiar are probably owls, including the eastern screech owl, which can be either gray or red; the common barn owl, with its ghostly face; and the great horned owl, which can reach 2 feet long with a wingspan of nearly 5 feet. Both barn owls and great horned owls range over much of the United States. There are also at least nine other owls that hide by day and feed by night. Other birds that live in open country—and can often be seen feeding in the moonlight on seeds or insects—are the northern mockingbird, a bird of desert, farm, wood, and suburb that often sings on warm moonlit nights, and the common nighthawk, a bird little seen by day but known to search the sky for insect food just after sunset and just before dawn. The nighthawk can be recognized by the sound it makes while diving—it sounds remarkably like a Bronx cheer. Other nocturnal birds include the chuck-will's-widow, a bird of the South that spends its day hiding in fallen leaves and nights searching for food. The whippoorwill is so nocturnal that it is chiefly known by its call.

The eastern screech owl, seen here in its red phase, is among the most common nocturnal birds in the eastern United States.

Flying squirrels are active at night, but you don't often see them. During the day, they sleep in hollow trees and abandoned birds' nests.

Bats

Bats have been the victims of a lot of bad press in this country. Long associated with things supernatural, they have also been accused of spreading rabies, tangling themselves in people's hair, and sucking blood. None of this is accurate.

The truth is, you are more likely to be struck by lightning than be bitten by a bat, and more likely to contract rabies from a neighborhood cat than from a bat. Bats simply have little interest in humans, and certainly have none in their hair. Even the notorious vampire bats prefer cows and chickens—and since they don't live in North America, the closest that you are likely to come to one is on a movie screen—or in your imagination.

Bats are unassuming creatures. Although to some people they resemble mice, they are mammals more closely related to human beings than to rodents. Tiny animals (the largest weighs less than two ounces), they spend most of their lives roosting, quietly resting, and hanging upside down in sheltered locations. During the day, bats go into "torpor," dropping their body temperature to conserve energy, then emerge at dusk to find a drink of water and feed.

Perhaps the bat's most remarkable characteristic is its navigational apparatus. Although they see perfectly well by day, bats like most animals have poor night vision. But by emitting bursts of sound as they fly through the evening sky, they create their own sonar, bouncing sounds off everything in their paths. This process, called echolating, allows bats to create a visual picture with sound, and navigate with ease around all obstacles to find their prey. It is a skill that the military can only envy.

Although three southwestern species feed on the nectar of night-blooming plants, the rest of the North American bats eat insects, voraciously. And for this they are worth their weight in gold to the savvy wildlife gardener. In warm weather, a single bat may eat hundreds of noxious night-flying insects an hour, including Japanese beetles, gypsy moths, flying ants, and other such pests.

Bats can be found in all 50 states. Of the 40 or so species spread across the country, the most common backyard bat is the red bat, a ravenous beetle-eater that looks something like a winged hamster. The tree-roosting hoary bat, second largest in North America, is also widespread. If you find a bat that has set up housekeeping in your attic or a corner of your porch, it is likely a big brown bat, the most common flying mammal in North America. Another species partial to houses is the little brown bat, found in the northern United States and Canada. The West and the Southwest are home to both the Mexican free-tail, which migrates southward during the winter (and is the bat found in New Mexico's Carlsbad Caverns), and the pallid bat, a blond creature with large ears, noted for pouncing on its prey on the ground.

The much-maligned bat is in fact a gardener's blessing. On a warm evening, a single bat can consume hundreds of noxious insects every hour.

Bat houses

A beginner's bat house can be assembled by almost anyone using about $10 worth of lumber, a sheet of fiberglass screening, plus a handsaw, a hammer, and a staple gun.

The bat house builder will need one stock piece of 8-foot 1" x 8" lumber (finish cut will be ¾" x 7½"), one 5' piece of 2" x 2" lumber (finish cut will be 1½" x 1½"), one 16½" piece of 1" x 4" lumber (finish cut will be ¾" x 3½") for the roof, and one 15½" x 23" piece of fiberglass screening (you must not use metal screening).

The lumber should be rough cut or grooved horizontally on one side, which should go on the inside of the finished bat house, so the bats will have something to hang on to.

Bats are very sensitive when it comes to the temperatures found in a bat house, so care must be taken not only in the final placement of the house but in the exterior finish used. In warmer climates, a bat house can be painted a medium brown or white and should have less than five hours of direct sunlight a day.

Houses mounted on poles offer the widest range of suitable temperatures, and the house should be located at least 15 to 20 feet above the ground. Although the sides of trees or buildings are also suitable places, in the northern part of the country, the shade provided by trees does not usually allow enough solar heating on cold winter days, so a building is often a better location. In moderate to cool climates, the house should face south or southeast so it absorbs at least five (preferably eight) hours of sunlight per day.

For more information on bat houses, write to Bat Conservation International, or the American Bat Conservation Society (See "Resources for wildlife gardeners" on page 187).

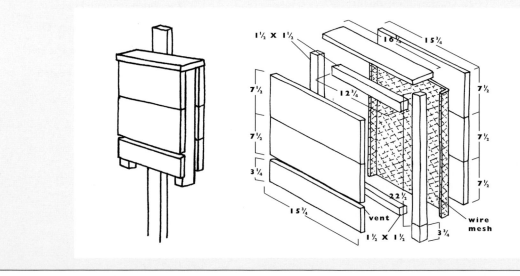

Flowers for the night garden

In order to open up the wildlife garden to nocturnal visitors, it's important to provide night-blooming flowers that attract moths and other insects. Once they arrive in numbers, the animals and other birds won't be far behind.

Moth flowers

There are major differences between day-blooming flowers and those that are open and fragrant at night. Because butterflies don't have a highly developed sense of smell, butterfly flowers have to rely on a visual appeal and are usually brightly colored. Their odor is also light and pleasant, and a number of these species such as heliotropes and roses form the base for many popular perfumes.

Flowers that attract nocturnal moths, by contrast, are usually white or pale yellow, and their perfume is strong and heady. Often the scent is almost *too* sweet, and it's usually slightly soapy. The flowers of the night-blooming ylang-ylang tree (*Cananga odorata*) are the base of Chanel No. 5 perfume. The fragrance of some of these flowers is so strong that they can be detected over great distances by the moths that visit and pollinate them.

Moth flowers are often tube-like in construction to perfectly accommodate the pollinator's very long proboscis, or tongue. In fact, moths have the longest tongues of any animals that visit flowers—some are a full foot long.

We recommend the following native American plants as a base for the nightlife garden. The biennial common evening primrose (*Oenothera biennis*) has pale yellow flowers that look worn and bedraggled by day but are fresh and fragrant at night. This biennial, hardy in Zones 4–9 and growing 3–5 feet tall, was introduced into gardens sometime in the eighteenth century as a root vegetable and for decades remained a popular ornamental. The flowers seem to open in slow motion, but when fully expanded they attract every moth in the neighborhood. There are now cultivars available that have larger flowers than the

Hooker's evening primrose (*Oenothera hookeri*) is a good choice for evening gardens in the western United States. Its yellow cup-shaped flowers are much like those of other evening primrose species.

species. Other wild members of the genus include the tufted evening primrose (*O. caespitosa*) of the Great Prairies, an 8-foot perennial that's hardy in Zones 4–7, and, throughout the West, Hooker's evening primrose (*O. hookeri*), growing 2 to 5 feet tall and hardy in Zones 5–10.

Yuccas (*Yucca* spp.) are noble American wildflowers that have sword-shaped leaves and bear huge upright clusters of hanging bell-like white blossoms by day. The blooms actually open wider at night and release vast amounts of a sweet scent in order to attract the yucca moth to aid in pollination. Adam's-needle (*Y. filamentosa*), a 5- to 15-foot perennial hardy in Zones 3–10, and soapweed (*Y. glauca*), growing 3 to 6 feet tall and hardy in Zones 3–10, are both large plants for the wild garden. The Spanish bayonet (*Y. baccata*), which grows 4 to 7 feet tall and is hardy in Zones 5–10, is another good choice.

Evening stars belong to the genus *Mentzelia*, and most are perennials from Texas, Colorado, and Nebraska. One of the best choices for the night garden is the star flower, stickleaf, or good woman (*M. nuda*), with small, Velcro-like hairs that cover the leaves and stick to passersby. These plants grow from 1 to 3 feet tall and are covered with pale yellow, starry flowers that open in the evening and close the following morning. Another excellent choice for the garden is the evening star (*M. decapetala*), which bears large, ten-petaled, creamy white star-like blossoms that open at sundown. This species grows 1 to 4 feet tall and is hardy in Zones 4–9.

Sweet-scented heliotrope is an American member of a genus that features the common heliotrope (*Heliotropium arborescens*), the extremely fragrant flower of summer borders. The American species is *H. convolvulaceum*, an annual growing up to 1 foot tall, and its species name refers to the fact that the white, very fragrant, funnel-shaped flowers look more like morning glories (which belong to the family *Convolvulaceae*) than any other flower. The plants come from the deserts of western Texas and extend their range to southeastern California, in Zones 9–11.

Other American wildflowers that bloom in the late afternoon and evening include sweet sand verbena (*Abronia fragrans*), 10 inches tall, native from Nebraska to Mexico and hardy in Zones 6–10, with stout stems that bear a multitude of blossoms exuding a sweet, vanilla-like fragrance; and southwestern ringstem (*Anulocaulis leisolenus*), a member of the four-o'clock family that produces white or pale pink flowers on top of 4-foot stems, which grows in southern Nevada, central Arizona, and western Texas, Zones 6–8. The desert lily (*Hesperocallis undulata*) has 2-foot stems that support 2-foot leaves with strongly waved edges and white funnel-shaped flowers that resemble Easter lilies (although open by day, they are most fragrant at night). It's hardy in Zones 9–10 and blooms in spring and summer.

You might also consider two night-blooming gauras—the scarlet gaura (*Gaura coccinea*) and the annual lizard-tail gaura (*G. parviflora*). Scarlet gaura is hardy in Zones 4–9, and its small, fragrant flowers open white, then turn pink and later scarlet as they age. Plants grow about 2 feet tall. Lizard-tail gaura can be grown for winter flowers in warm-climate gardens in the Southwest. Its flowers are pink to rose-colored, on plants growing 1 to 5 feet high.

The four-o'clock (*Mirabilis jalapa*) is a tender perennial from South America that has long been grown as an annual in North America. Its red, pink, yellow, or white flowers open late in the afternoon and often stay open all night. A relative native to American prairies, desert four-o'clock (*Mirabilis multiflora*) is hardy in Zones 5–9 and has rosy purple flowers. A single plant may be 4 feet across and 20 inches tall.

Finally, for sheer evening drama, there are the moonflowers (*Ipomoea alba*), tropical perennials that do beautifully in most American gardens when grown as annuals. Moonflowers are a type of morning glory, and the vines, which may reach 20 feet in frost-free areas, bloom in mid- to late summer from seeds sown in spring. The large, sweetly fragrant white flowers open in the early evening and are favorite haunts of a number of species of moths.

Chapter Nine

Profiles of 15 NWF Backyard Habitats

Now join us on a stroll through this remarkable gallery of 15 certified **NWF Backyard Habitats**. As you page through, one thing will strike you over and over—these habitats work! They not only look great, but they attract all sorts of fascinating wild creatures. Birds enjoy a variety of feeders, and flowers have been chosen to nourish butterflies and hummingbirds. From New Hampshire and Virginia to Oregon and California, from 10,000 square feet to more than 11 acres, these habitats will inspire you with their diversity.

This landscape just outside Madison, Wisconsin, looks more like an English garden than a wildlife haven. The lush garden, which is a third of an acre, is especially surprising because the climate is a cold USDA Zone 4. The front of the house features a small front lawn shaded by a 'Greenspire' linden tree and a 'Zumi' crabapple. Virginia creeper and trumpet vine cloak a chain-link fence. Where other people grow grass, the owners have planted a prairie garden, wildflower collections, and a few more conventional garden perennials to enhance the colorful display. ◆ In this habitat, plant species number in the hundreds. Among the more unusual plants are black snakeroot, rattlesnake master, and two wild grapevines. The owners have planted many species in large groups of a single type of plant, for an attractive massed look reminiscent of the drift style of planting found in English beds and borders. ◆ Their trees are also diverse, including Norway spruces, Austrian pines, and a choice selection of small trees. And the yard has many shrubs, featuring lilacs and three species of dogwoods. There is also a host of other trees and shrubs that produce berries, seeds, or fruit for the birds. ◆ The property is regularly visited by wrens, hummingbirds, woodpeckers, juncos, chickadeees, sparrows, indigo buntings, and sharp-shinned hawks, as well as squirrels, rabbits, chipmunks, and moles.

Shade-loving wildflowers, ferns, and perennials (with a pot of lantana added for color) provide a lush understory for trees and shrubs that shelter birds.

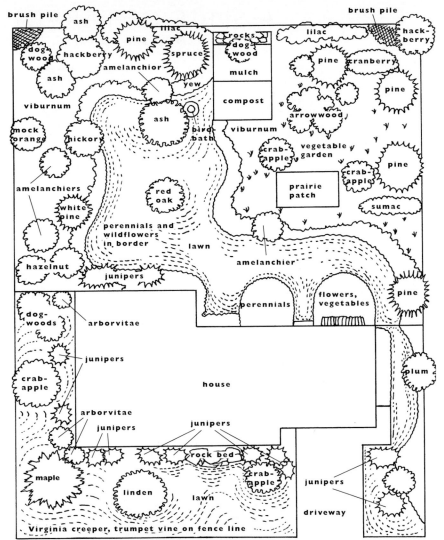

brush pile

ash

dog wood

hackberry

ash

viburnum

amelanchior

lilac

pine

spruce

yew

ash

bird bath

mock orange

hickory

amelanchiers

white pine

red oak

perennials and wildflowers in border

hazelnut

junipers

lawn

amelanchier

rocks dog wood

mulch

compost

viburnum

lilac

hackberry

brush pile

pine

cranberry

pine

arrowwood

crabapple

vegetable garden

crabapple

pine

prairie patch

sumac

pine

perennials

flowers, vegetables

dogwoods

arborvitae

junipers

crabapple

arborvitae

junipers

junipers

rock bed

crabapple

junipers

driveway

pine

plum

house

maple

linden

lawn

Virginia creeper, trumpet vine on fence line

A meadow border in full bloom bursts with the color of scarlet bee balm, pink bergamot, and other wildflowers.

A SLICE OF PARADISE
Minnesota

It gets cold in Minnesota, sometimes -30°F, but the owners still call their backyard garden in Minneapolis a "Slice of Paradise." Judging by the birds that flock to the formidable array of feeders, the word has gotten around in the bird community that this home is a good place to visit. ◆ The house looks out on a view of a city park. It sits about midway in a lot that measures 125 feet long and 43 feet wide (0.12 acre). It features an elevated balcony where the owner stands with his spotting scope, checking out the day's birds. The property has a small front lawn that takes just ten minutes to mow. The lawn has an irregular outline due to the rock garden, the herb bed, and the hedgerow that surround it. ◆ For the butterflies, there are plenty of prairie flowers—prairies having been the original Minnesota habitat. For the birds, there are nesting boxes, plus water all year. There are trumpet vines for the hummingbirds and a bat house for the bats, too. ◆ The habitat has lots of trees for shade and shelter, both coniferous and deciduous. In addition, there is a privacy screen of Lombardy poplars along one side of the front edge of the lot, and a tight hedgerow on the other. A compost silo is shaded by a 60-foot catalpa tree, and from its base you can look over at a raspberry patch, a wild grape arbor, a vegetable garden, a solar greenhouse, and a nest box for the local screech owls.

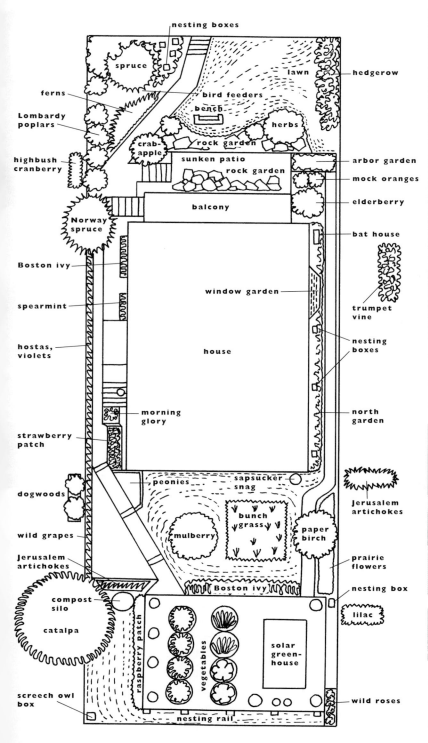

nesting boxes

spruce

ferns

Lombardy
poplars

highbush
cranberry

Norway
spruce

Boston ivy

spearmint

hostas,
violets

strawberry
patch

dogwoods

wild grapes

Jerusalem
artichokes

compost
silo

catalpa

screech owl
box

lawn

bird feeders

bench

herbs

crab-
apple

rock garden

sunken patio

rock garden

balcony

window garden

house

morning
glory

peonies

sapsucker
snag

mulberry

bunch
grass

raspberry patch

vegetables

solar
green-
house

nesting rail

Boston ivy

hedgerow

arbor garden

mock oranges

elderberry

bat house

trumpet
vine

nesting
boxes

north
garden

Jerusalem
artichokes

paper
birch

prairie
flowers

nesting box

lilac

wild roses

This birdhouse is well hidden during the nesting season by the deciduous vines covering the wall.

Be sure to keep ground-level feeders cleared of snow and ice and stocked with food throughout the winter.

A HIDDEN HABITAT
Wisconsin

Here is another property in Wisconsin devoted to wildlife, but this one-acre lot enjoys a USDA Zone 5 climate because it's close to the shores of Lake Michigan. However, it fronts a busy street, so in order to cut back on noise pollution, the owners have cleverly constructed 5-foot-high earth berms to muffle street sounds. The berms are bordered with cattails, common milkweed, and Russian olives. ◆ On the house side of the berms, there are over 20 white pines, then a natural area of prairie that is planted with wildflowers while the small woodland develops. In the back of the property is a standing water swale with marsh marigolds, elderberry bushes, and viburnums, as well as a small pond, providing local and migrating wildlife with much-needed water. It is backed by another triangular-shaped prairie garden with two bur oaks at its edge. The prairie garden in bloom is a particularly beautiful sight, with coneflowers and black-eyed Susans growing in the midst of thousands of big and little bluestem grasses. It effectively refutes the argument that grass exists only to be cut. ◆ Six bird feeders distribute suet, seeds, and fruit to birds that include sapsuckers, downy woodpeckers, chickadees, juncos, goldfinches, Baltimore orioles, and blackbirds. There are also rock piles and rock walls, log piles, and hidden brush piles where wildlife can nest and find shelter.

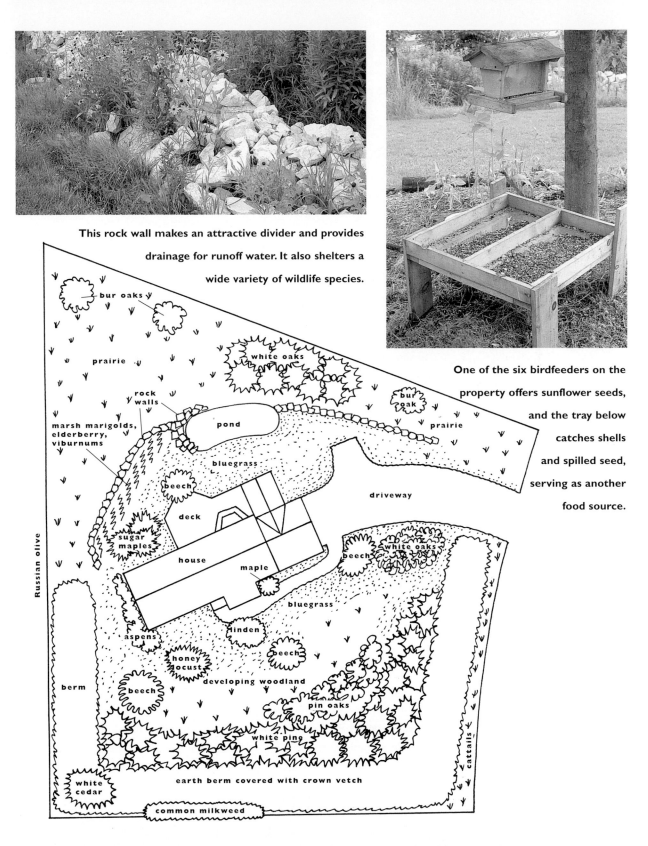

This rock wall makes an attractive divider and provides drainage for runoff water. It also shelters a wide variety of wildlife species.

One of the six birdfeeders on the property offers sunflower seeds, and the tray below catches shells and spilled seed, serving as another food source.

bur oaks

prairie

white oaks

rock walls

bur oak

prairie

marsh marigolds, elderberry, viburnums

pond

bluegrass

driveway

beech

deck

white oaks

Russian olive

sugar maples

house

beech

maple

bluegrass

aspens

linden

beech

berm

honey locust

developing woodland

beech

pin oaks

white pine

cattails

white cedar

earth berm covered with crown vetch

common milkweed

A FRESH MEADOW MARSH
Pennsylvania

Nine years ago, a couple yearning for the country bought an 11.4-acre lot that had been a Bucks County cornfield. Today, that property boasts seven ponds of various sizes plus a small bog and marsh, and the owners are creating a freshwater meadow by planting their own rushes without waiting for nature to do the job. Cattails and arrowhead also accent the water garden. ◆ Because the land is located on a flyway between two local parks, these gardens continually host a number of migrant waterfowl in addition to the year-round avian residents. In the winter, a recirculating pump keeps some of the water free of ice. ◆ Three hanging feeders holding niger seed, millet, and a songbird seed mix—and four ground feeders full of sunflower seeds and corn—attract finches, sparrows, mourning doves, cardinals, cowbirds, and redwing blackbirds. Hummingbird feeders containing sugar water lure hummers to the garden in summer. ◆ The trees include oaks, maples, hybrid poplars, and crabapples. There are wild rosebushes, dogwoods, and a host of annuals and perennials for added color. Evergreens include white pines, hemlocks, and arborvitae. There are also pussywillows, trumpet vines, and honeysuckles. ◆ The owners know that spring has finally arrived when the killdeer come back, swallows start to skim the pond, and a mallard settles in to raise her brood.

A trio of duck houses in a pond provides welcome nesting space for waterfowl.

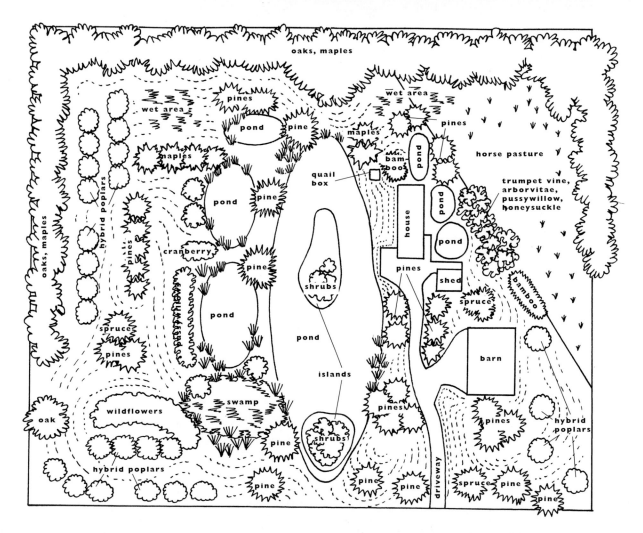

oaks, maples

wet area

oaks, maples

pines

pond

pine

wet area

pines

maples

maples

horse pasture

bamboo

pond

quail box

pond

pine

house

pond

trumpet vine, arborvitae, pussywillow, honeysuckle

hybrid poplars

pond

cranberry

pine

pond

shrubs

shed

pines

spruce

bamboo

pond

spruce

pines

islands

barn

pines

shrubs

wildflowers

swamp

pine

oak

pines

hybrid poplars

shrubs

hybrid poplars

pine

pine

pine

pines

spruce

pine

driveway

hybrid poplars

pine

pine

A COMPACT BIRD SANCTUARY
Pennsylvania

On a 65 × 90-foot lot near Bristol, Pennsylvania, there's a straw nesting house that looks like an architect's plan for a Baltimore oriole's home. But that's not the only sign that birds are welcome at this property. Birdbaths and feeders are everywhere, and they're especially appropriate since the owners live across the street from a nature center and next door to a woods that includes all sorts of nature trails. Nesting boxes and bird houses are home to both wrens and bluebirds, and bats, too, are welcome in this garden. ◆ The front yard is ringed with a privacy fence, and there is a small pond near the center of the lawn. The water in the pond is kept in continual motion by a small fountain made of metal lily pads. Real water lilies, many water lettuce plants, and striped rushes are reflected in the pond's ripples by day and lit by low-voltage lighting by night. ◆ It's a small lot, but it is full of plant life, including a large maple, dogwoods, white pines, and cherries along the line that separates the lot from a roadway along one side. The many shrubs include low-growing hollies, raspberries, lilac bushes, azaleas (which the owners prize for their spring flowers), and more evergreens. ◆ On the front deck, next to a comfortable green Adirondack chair, sits a large concrete cocker spaniel. Man's best friend is there to welcome rather than to disturb the feathered visitors.

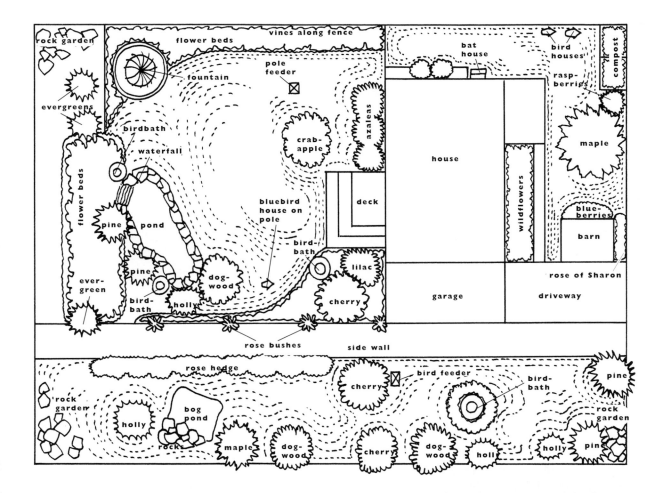

rock garden

vines along fence

flower beds

bird houses

bat house

compost

fountain

pole feeder

raspberries

evergreens

azaleas

maple

birdbath

crab-apple

waterfall

house

flower beds

wildflowers

pine

pond

blue-berries

deck

pine

bluebird house on pole

barn

ever-green

bird-bath

dog-wood

bird-bath

lilac

rose of Sharon

bird-bath

holly

cherry

garage

driveway

rose bushes

side wall

rose hedge

bird feeder

bird-bath

pine

rock garden

cherry

rock garden

holly

bog pond

rocks

maple

dog-wood

cherry

dog-wood

holly

holly

pine

Left: A nesting house of woven straw resembles an oriole's nest, and provides elegant accomodations for avian tenants.

Right: The water in this small pool is kept in continuous gentle motion by a small fountain.

AN ACRE FOR WILDLIFE
Virginia

Not far from the beltway in Washington, D.C., out in the county of Arlington, Virginia, there is a one-acre lot that enjoys a climate where winter temperatures rarely fall below zero. Situated almost in the middle of the lot is a small, rustic, dark brown clapboard cottage with a wide front porch screened with wisteria vines. It's the type of cottage that some of the earliest settlers used, and you can almost imagine being in the Virginia of 100 years ago. ◆ The small lawn is surrounded by groundcovers and patches of variegated hostas. Small fountains of liriope share space with azaleas, pachysandra, and andromeda. All the plantings are carefully mulched with pine needles for an entirely natural look. ◆ The owners provide water year-round, bird feeders, and plenty of places for wildlife to hide, including dense scrub areas, piles of logs, and groundcovers like the pachysandra and beds of English ivy. ◆ For overhead protection, there is a star magnolia (15 feet high and 10 feet wide), as well as hickories, mulberries, cedars, white pines, oaks, and hemlocks. ◆ A stone-lined pool is surrounded by summer annuals with plenty of red flowers, including impatiens and red salvias, to attract hummingbirds. Among the many birds that visit the property are goldfinches, house finches, cardinals, chickadees, and woodpeckers. Squirrels and chipmunks are welcome, too.

Neatly mulched plantings of liriope, hostas, groundcovers, azaleas, and other shrubs surround the lawn. Birdhouses and feeders are installed in the trees.

In this corner of the garden, birds find food, water, and shelter together in one area. Red and orange impatiens and other annuals surrounding the pool attract hummingbirds.

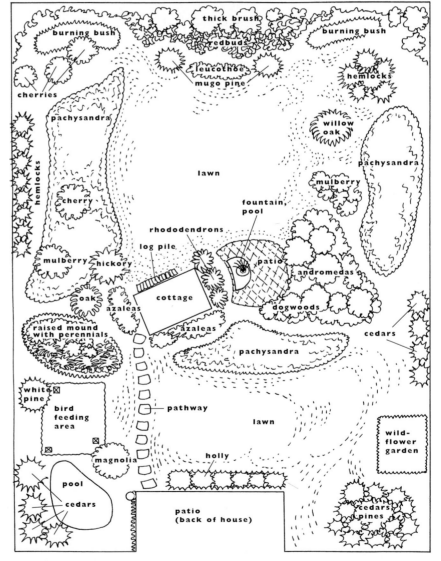

thick brush

burning bush

redbuds

burning bush

leucothoe

cherries

mugo pine

hemlocks

pachysandra

willow oak

hemlocks

pachysandra

cherry

mulberry

fountain, pool

rhododendrons

log pile

mulberry

hickory

patio

andromedas

oak

azaleas

cottage

dogwoods

cedars

raised mound with perennials

azaleas

pachysandra

white pine

bird feeding area

pathway

lawn

wild-flower garden

magnolia

holly

pool

cedars

patio (back of house)

cedars pines

A BAYSIDE HABITAT
Maryland

Right on the Chesapeake Bay, on Maryland's Eastern Shore, is a two-story white frame house surrounded by a rectangular 10,000-square-foot plot of land. It's amazing just how many plants can be packed into such a small space. This garden holds over 30 large trees, 15 small trees, and over 60 shrubs. ◆ One long edge of the rectangle consists of a planting of daylilies and iris in front, then a line of Leyland cypresses that stop just before a storage shed, with a large fig tree as the end of that line. ◆ The opposite edge of the rectangle consists of fruit trees (including apples, pears, and plums), oaks, roses of Sharon, and Canadian hemlocks. These are underplanted with shade-loving wildflowers,

perennials, and low shrubs: sweet woodruff, spiderwort, hostas, ferns, mayapples, Jack-in-the-pulpit, lilies-of-the-valley, and azaleas. Sun-loving perennials include lady's mantle, daylilies, yuccas, and Russian sage. ◆ In the backyard, there are over 30 cultivars of roses, three small vegetable gardens, a grape arbor, and a small perennial bed, with butterfly bushes and burning bush underplanted with coreopsis and poppies. ◆ The owners provide water year-round, including a birdbath with dripping water and a small pond that can be easily seen from their backyard patio. In addition to the standard birds, red-winged blackbirds, grackles, and cowbirds are among the visitors.

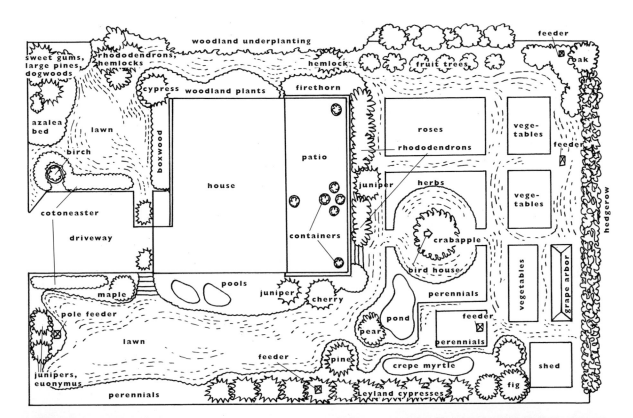

woodland underplanting   feeder

sweet gums, large pines, dogwoods   rhododendrons, hemlocks   hemlock   fruit trees   oak

cypress   woodland plants   firethorn

azalea bed   lawn

birch

boxwood

patio   roses   rhododendrons   vegetables

feeder

cotoneaster

house

juniper   herbs   vegetables

driveway   containers   crabapple

bird house   vegetables   grape arbor

hedgerow

maple   pools   juniper   cherry   perennials

pole feeder   pear   pond   feeder

lawn   perennials

junipers, euonymus   feeder   pine   crepe myrtle   shed

perennials   Leyland cypresses   fig

This small pool, bordered by rocks and surrounded by a lovely mix of perennials, can be seen from the house.

A mixed border of shrubs and perennials provides shelter, cover, and berries for food.

Gardening for Wildlife **167**

A HOTBED OF BIRDS AND BUTTERFLIES
Georgia

Just north of Atlanta is a half-acre garden where temperatures rarely go below 10°F in winter, but the summers can be very hot indeed. In spite of the hot weather, behind the house the owners have created a yard meant for wildlife. The yard contains a small pond, various raised beds under a canopy of native dogwoods, American beeches, and eastern white pines. ◆ Behind the patio is a charming screened gazebo, from which the owners can comfortably watch the butterflies and birds fly among the flowers. The wildlife-wise owners make sure that the plants are chosen not only for the adult butterflies but for their caterpillars, too. The plants include passionflowers to feed the occasional tropical and semi-tropical visitors like the gulf fritillary, and thistles for the painted ladies. Other butterfly flowers include coral bells, phlox, Russian sage, sweet William, butterfly weed, and cardinal flower. There is also a sizable wildflower meadow. ◆ Birds can find sources of water all year. The garden has birdbaths, seed feeders, nectar feeders, and one suet feeder. The bird visitors include cardinals, finches, siskins, bluebirds, titmice, woodpeckers, and ruby-throated hummingbirds. ◆ Additional food for birds is provided by a number of berry-bearing shrubs. There are also nesting boxes, trees with nesting cavities, and log and brush piles to provide shelter for birds and animals.

Left: Flat rocks edging a small pool provide perches on which birds and small animals can rest to take a drink.

Right: The red berries of a hybrid holly offer a bounty of food for birds. The cotoneasters below also produce berries that many birds favor.

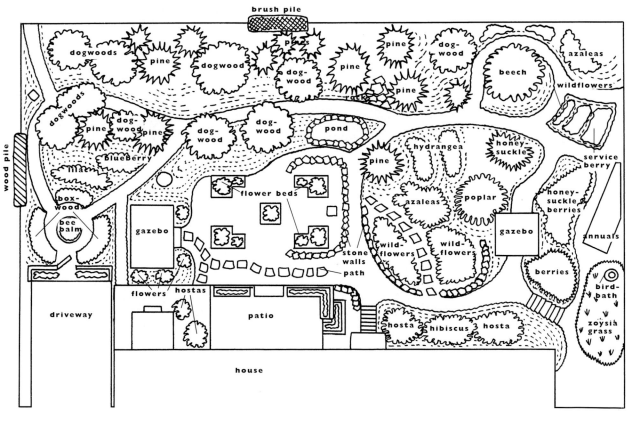

brush pile

dogwoods
pine
dogwood
pines
pine
dog-wood
dog-wood
pine
pine
beech
azaleas
wildflowers

dogwoods
pine
dog-wood
pine
dog-wood
dog-wood
rocks
pond
pine
hydrangea
honey-suckle
service berry

blueberry
flower beds
azaleas
poplar
honey-suckle berries

box-woods
bee balm
gazebo
stone walls path
wild-flowers
wild-flowers
gazebo
annuals
berries

flowers
hostas
hosta
hibiscus
hosta
bird-bath
zoysia grass

driveway
patio

wood pile

house

PETER LOEWER'S GARDEN
North Carolina

Not far from Asheville's city center, amid the Great Smoky Mountains, this one-acre garden fronts on the shore of an artificial lake created some 65 years ago. When the lot was developed, all the original trees were left, including seven varied oak trees, a grove of dogwoods, a very old white pine, and a tulip poplar. Over the years seedling trees have appeared, and now two new tulip poplars, one American witch hazel, a grove of honey locusts, and a sourwood tree have joined the collection. ◆ The winters occasionally reach a few degrees below zero, but the southern sun soon coaxes snowdrops to bloom in February. Except on very frigid nights, the garden's wildlife is usually active most of the year. Even though the garden is within the city limits, raccoons, opossums, two red foxes, chipmunks, and squirrels (including gray and flying squirrels) make their homes in the high oaks. The nearby lake attracts migratory ducks to spend most of the colder months in residence—even in the coldest winters, a nearby inlet never freezes. ◆ The perennial garden is planted for butterflies, and there are bird feeders throughout the woods and on the back terrace to provide nourishment all winter long and throughout most of the summer. Visitors include chickadees, Carolina wrens, titmice, cardinals, song and chipping sparrows, and many migratory birds that pass by in spring and fall.

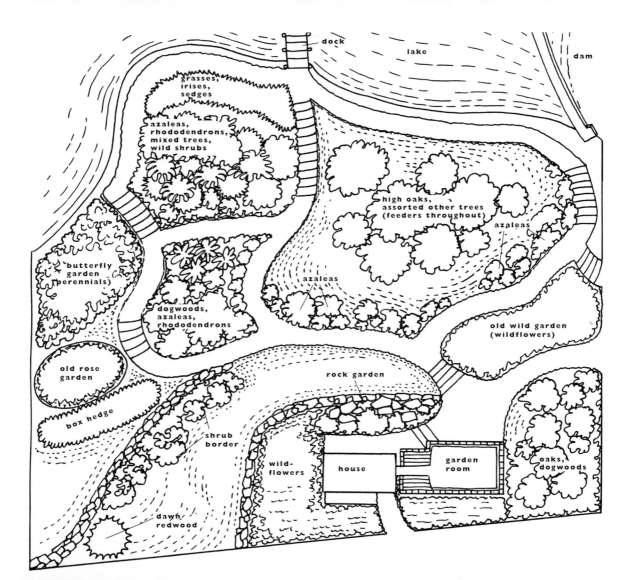

grasses, irises, sedges

azaleas, rhododendrons, mixed trees, wild shrubs

dock

lake

dam

high oaks, assorted other trees (feeders throughout)

azaleas

azaleas

butterfly garden (perennials)

dogwoods, azaleas, rhododendrons

old wild garden (wildflowers)

old rose garden

rock garden

box hedge

shrub border

wild-flowers

house

garden room

oaks, dogwoods

dawn redwood

Left: A flagstone path leads into the woods, where bird feeders are kept filled throughout the year.

Right: Joe-Pye weed is one of the perennials planted to attract butterflies, and these swallowtails find it attractive.

A BUSY BIRD GARDEN
South Carolina

The summers are hot in Columbia, South Carolina. But on this small 17,000-square-foot parcel, a cooling canopy of oaks, pines, winged elms, sweet gums, and red maples provides a wildlife garden just for the birds. The owners supply water year-round with several birdbaths, a pool filled with water lilies, and a wandering stream. Hollies, wax myrtles, dogwoods, redbuds and plum trees are among the smaller trees that dot the property. ◆ Feeders include a thistle feeder, suet baskets, and two hummingbird feeders. They attract cardinals, chickadees, bluejays, purple finches, house finches, woodpeckers, thrashers, robins, titmice, and black-birds. A dense shrubbery of red tip and Japanese privet (both of which are well adapted to drought, heat, and cold), extensive plantings of nandina (heavenly bamboo), and many azaleas provide additional cover for the birds. ◆ A deck at the rear of the house is covered with pots planted with geraniums. Behind the pool is a small arbor and seating area sufficiently removed from the house for birdwatching. There, the owners can look out on a young redbud tree, the vegetable garden, or the many perennial plantings that feature daylilies, sunflowers, coreopsis, mums, and roses. Additional benches are located throughout the garden.

This raised, terraced pool edged with rocks is a great source of water for birds.

A cardinal visits a feeder containing sunflower seeds and, on the left, a suet basket.

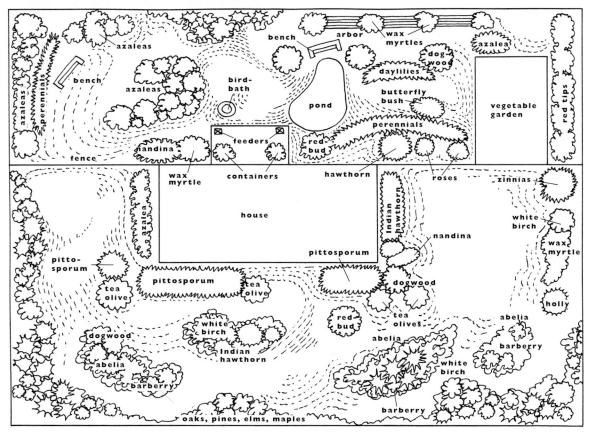

A BIRDER'S DREAM
Massachusetts

It's called "Joan's Birdlist," and it includes all the birds that visit a 19,000-square-foot plot less than 20 miles from Boston. While close enough to the Atlantic for warming trends, the garden is still vulnerable to winters with -10°F lows. But in this wildlife garden with jet trails overhead, the habitat includes a scrub patch, a garden pond, mature trees, wildflowers, perennials, and an adjacent wetland. Large trees include white pines, maples, and one mountain ash. There are a number of small trees and shrubs, but the major plant species consist of over 80 perennials and annuals in various combinations around the property. ◆ The owner's lifelist of birds includes seasonal visits from the Baltimore (or northern) oriole, the common northern flicker, the common nighthawk, the glorious wood thrush, the red-bellied woodpecker, and the Carolina wren. In fact, this list chronicles the coming and going of over 80 birds, some common but many rare. ◆ The pond is situated so that wildlife residents always feel secure. Green frogs, leopard frogs, and salamanders are counted as regular seasonal residents, along with turtles, toads, and an occasional ribbon or garter snake. ◆ Animals have included the little brown bat, raccoons, rabbits, skunks, the short-tailed shrew, meadow voles, and, of all things, a Canadian lynx (or bobcat) that had strayed too far east from its Adirondack home.

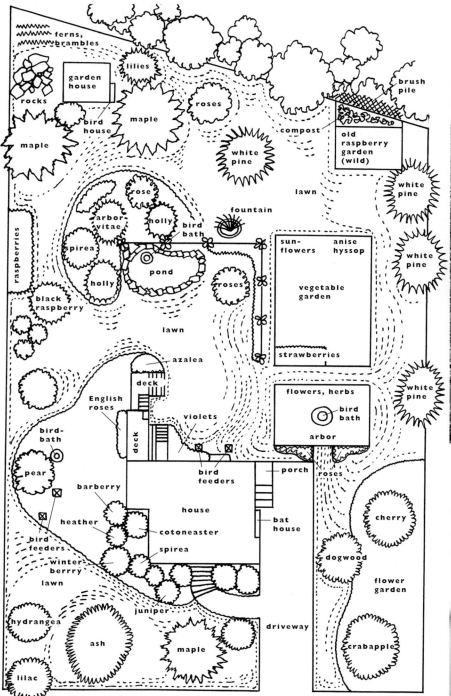

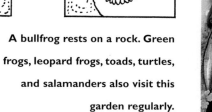

In the wetland, a bird house mounted atop a pole stands amid cattails, goldenrod, and a variety of other moisture-loving plants.

A bullfrog rests on a rock. Green frogs, leopard frogs, toads, turtles, and salamanders also visit this garden regularly.

A DIVERSE STREAM GARDEN
Oregon

Portland, Oregon, is a city with a view, and the owners of a 12,500 square foot lot are blessed with plenty of rain and winters where temperatures rarely fall below freezing. A small, and rippling, rocky rill winds its way through the yard, bordered with azaleas, sedums, and Irish and Scotch mosses. ◆ Rhododendrons and azaleas grow brilliantly in the Pacific Northwest, and this garden is no exception. But there are also firs, a large-leaf maple, hazelnuts, and a Japanese black pine. For smaller trees, the owners chose kousa or Chinese dogwoods, a Japanese snowbell, Pacific dogwoods, and a lovely white birch. ◆ Platform feeders (one with black oil sunflowers and one with chicken scratch), two large hanging feeders, and a tube feeder featuring niger seed, plus the stream and the pond, provide both water and food year-round. Visiting birds have included pine siskins, chickadees, finches, nuthatches, towhees, juncos, and jays. ◆ In addition, the garden features a number of nesting boxes and nesting shelves, and dens in both ground and rock. A butterfly garden with various perennials is situated next to the rear deck, and a compost pile is carefully screened by snowberry and blackberry bushes. Winding paths edged with stone wander throughout the garden, giving the landscape a natural look—but the hands of the gardeners are in evidence as well.

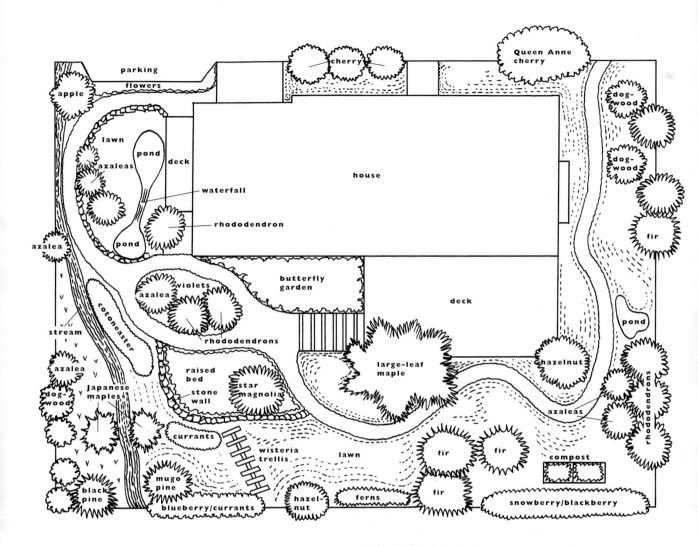

parking
flowers

apple

lawn

azaleas

pond

deck

waterfall

rhododendron

pond

azalea

cotoneaster

stream

azalea

violets

azalea

rhododendrons

dog-wood

Japanese maples

raised bed

stone wall

star magnolia

currants

wisteria trellis

black pine

mugo pine

blueberry/currants

hazel-nut

ferns

lawn

butterfly garden

large-leaf maple

cherry

Queen Anne cherry

dog-wood

dog-wood

fir

house

deck

pond

hazelnut

azaleas

rhododendrons

fir

fir

fir

compost

snowberry/blackberry

A colorful raised-bed flower garden full of annuals is contained by a dry stone wall that's full of nooks and crannies for small plants and wildlife.

A TROPICAL GARDEN
California

While the birds that visit this garden not too far from the warm Pacific are rarely tropical, the plants here certainly are. In this 3,500-square-foot garden, the temperatures rarely go below freezing. The wildlife garden features two banana plants, one Brazilian pepper, and a number of exotic tree ferns and other heat-loving fern species. ◆ In this garden cordyline can reach a height of 10 feet. In a bed surrounded by stone and concrete, tall Swiss-cheese plants send their aerial roots twining around each other and out on the pathways, while goldfish wind through the sparkling waters with their otherworldly tropical water lilies on a year-round basis. Other "houseplants" that grow outside include Kaffir lilies, bougainvilleas, blood lilies, and lots of begonias, fuchsias, and even a few orchids. Mature trees include pines, a sycamore, and a large silk oak, while a dense grove of bamboos adds a more tropical touch. ◆ The hummingbird population loves the tropical flowers and includes many species common in the West but rarely seen east of the Mississippi, like Anna's and Costa's hummingbirds. Bird feeders with mixed seed are hosts to many sparrows, house finches, and the ubiquitous mourning doves. The waterfalls and small birdbaths are popular with all the visiting birds.

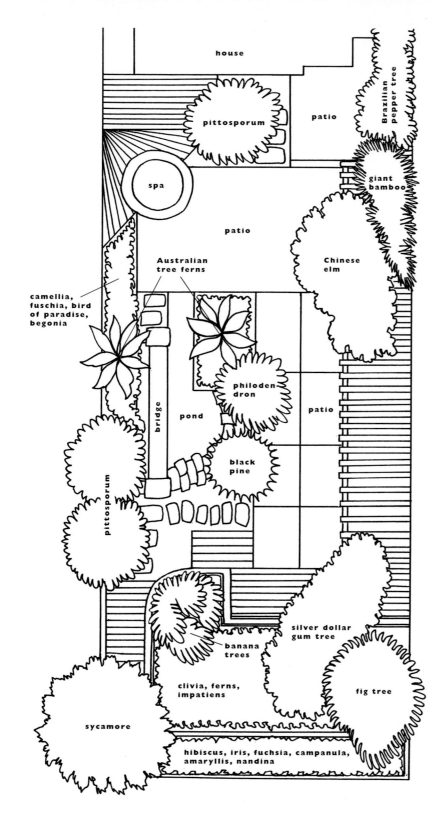

house

pittosporum

patio

Brazilian pepper tree

spa

giant bamboo

patio

Chinese elm

Australian tree ferns

camellia, fuschia, bird of paradise, begonia

philoden dron

bridge

pond

patio

pittosporum

black pine

banana trees

silver dollar gum tree

clivia, ferns, impatiens

fig tree

sycamore

hibiscus, iris, fuchsia, campanula, amaryllis, nandina

This small pond is home to goldfish and is a source of water for birds and other creatures.

Hummingbirds are drawn to the many tropical red and orange flowers in the garden.

This small wild garden is just east of the New York border and about ten miles north of the Connecticut shoreline. In winter it enjoys the warming effects of Long Island Sound. The land in this garden totals just over 2 acres, and it features a large pond with a water area that covers a half-acre. ◆ The view from the front of the house is beautiful. Over an acre of the land is covered by large trees, including various oaks, hickories, and maples. The smaller trees include serviceberries, alders, rhododendrons, arborvitae, elderberries, and mountain ashes. ◆ Among the array of bird feeders is an automatic type with a built-in baffle to exclude marauding squirrels. The birds that visit this rural retreat number over 100 and include yellow warblers, catbirds, flycatchers, woodpeckers, mockingbirds, house wrens, and hummingbirds. ◆ Groundcover plantings incorporate junipers, yews, and rockspray cotoneasters, plus dogwoods, raspberries, and blackberries. In addition, there are American bittersweet vines, wild grapes, and honeysuckles. ◆ Around the pond are extensive plantings of tall grasses, cattails, and a number of wild sedges, their reflections adding to the beauty of the water garden. Wildflowers abound, including Joe-Pye weed, milkweed, and pearly everlasting. This area is off limits to household pets, but not to the many waterfowl and other wildlife visitors that make frequent stops there.

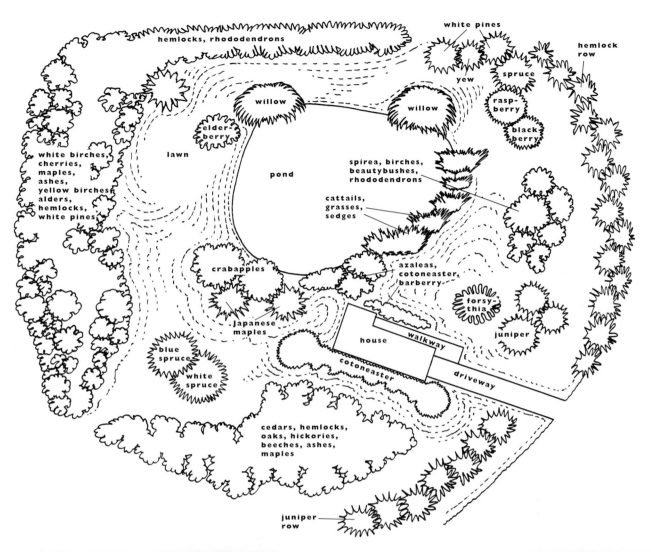

white pines

hemlocks, rhododendrons

hemlock row

yew

spruce

willow

willow

raspberry

elderberry

black berry

lawn

white birches, cherries, maples, ashes, yellow birches alders, hemlocks, white pines

spirea, birches, beautybushes, rhododendrons

pond

cattails, grasses, sedges

crabapples

azaleas, cotoneaster, barberry

forsythia

Japanese maples

juniper

blue spruce

house

walkway

white spruce

cotoneaster

driveway

cedars, hemlocks, oaks, hickories, beeches, ashes, maples

juniper row

Left: Turtles use a well-placed tree branch as their own private bridge and dock.

Right: Rockspray cotoneaster and juniper planted as groundcovers behind the house provide berries in fall and winter.

ON THE EDGE OF THE WOODS
New Hampshire

In what is just about the geographic center of New Hampshire, not too far from Hillsboro, winter temperatures often plunge to -25°F. Here, there is a wildlife garden of four acres surrounded by woods. Even the herb garden and the rock garden are backed by a diorama of trees. ◆ Large trees are represented by both red and white oaks, white pines, Canadian hemlocks, paper birch, American beech, and both sugar and red maples. Smaller trees include crabapples, dogwoods, Japanese maples, redbuds, a weeping peach, and a weeping cherry. Shrubs include mountain laurels, blueberries, rugosa or Japanese roses, elderberries, serviceberries, mock oranges, and a beautybush. ◆ There are a number of annuals and perennials for butterflies; they range from tithonias to asters, cosmos, and dahlias. In the herb garden, parsley and caraway are planted to nourish black swallowtail caterpillars. ◆ Although a variety of animals visit this garden, the emphasis is on birds. By using tube feeders stocked with niger, oil sunflower seed, cracked corn, white millet, and peanuts, the owners enjoy a variety of birds. Frequent visitors include both downy and hairy woodpeckers, chickadees, nuthatches, tufted titmice, juncos, and evening grosbeaks. Nesting boxes provide sites for tree swallows and purple martins. Seasonal water is provided by a dripping hose and two garden pools.

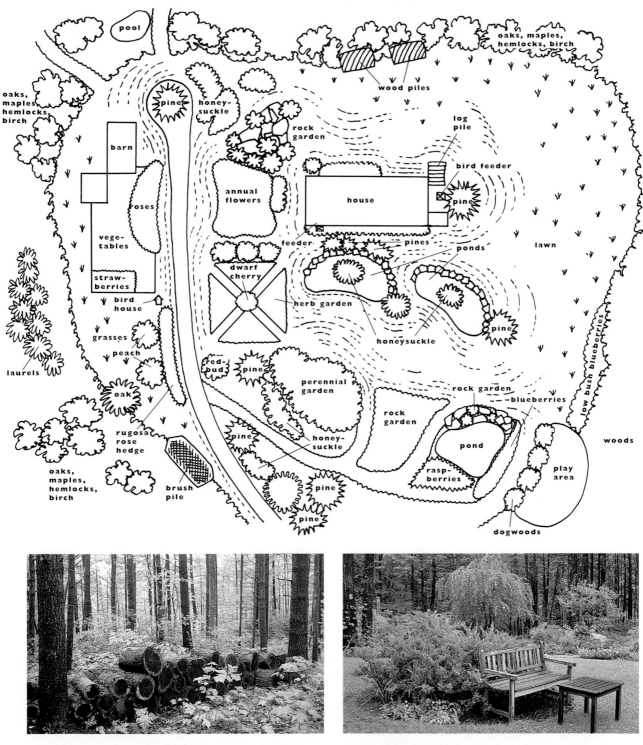

Labels within the diagram:

pool

oaks, maples, hemlocks, birch

oaks, maples hemlocks, birch

wood piles

pine

honey-suckle

rock garden

log pile

barn

bird feeder

annual flowers

house

pine

roses

feeder

pines

ponds

lawn

vege-tables

dwarf cherry

herb garden

straw-berries

honeysuckle

pine

bird house

grasses

laurels

peach

red-bud

pine

perennial garden

rock garden

rock garden

blueberries

oak

honey-suckle

pond

low bush blueberries

rugosa rose hedge

pine

raspberries

play area

woods

oaks, maples, hemlocks, birch

brush pile

pine

pine

dogwoods

Neat wood piles separate lawn area from woods and offer shelter to small creatures.

A bench allows the gardeners to sit quietly and observe the visiting wildlife.

BACKYARD WILDLIFE HABITAT PROGRAM
APPLICATION • FOR • CERTIFICATION

NAME _____

ADDRESS _____

CITY _____ COUNTY _____

STATE/PROVINCE _____ ZIP/POSTAL CODE _____

TELEPHONE _____

PROPERTY SIZE (Sq. Ft. or Acres) _____

HABITAT # _____

OFFICE USE:
fee rcvd. —
certified —
c.s. —
key words —

HAVE YOU EVER APPLIED FOR CERTIFICATION BEFORE ___ YES ___ NO IF YES LIST STATE OR HABITAT NO. _____

Take heart, you needn't be a zoologist or botanist to fill out this application. We're anxious to reward your efforts in providing habitat for wildlife where you live or work as soon as we can. Do the best you can to fill out the application—if there are problems with it (and there rarely are) we'll get back to you with some suggestions. Within 4-6 weeks of receiving your application we'll forward to you a beautiful personalized certificate suitable for framing.

1. FOOD/*Plantings and Feeders*

A. Do your best to list those plants on your property which might provide wildlife foods such as acorns, berries, nuts, seeds, buds or nectar.

LARGE TREES	NO.	SMALL TREES	NO.	SHRUBS	NO.	ANNUALS & PERENNIALS	NO.

B. List the type and number of feeders and foods that you provide for wildlife.

FEEDER TYPE	NO.	FOODS	VISITED BY

2. WATER/*Drinking, Bathing*

A. We provide water: ☐ Year Round ☐ Seasonally

B. We provide water in the following ways:
☐ Bird Bath ☐ Water dripping into a bird bath
☐ Spring ☐ Wildlife Pool ☐ Pond ☐ Stream
☐ Other _____

Working for the Nature of Tomorrow®
NATIONAL WILDLIFE FEDERATION 1400 Sixteenth Street, N.W., Washington, D.C. 20036-2266

3. COVER/*Places to Hide*

A. We provide wind and weather breaks and places for wildlife to hide from predators in the following manner.

☐ Dense Shrubs (which types?) _____

☐ Evergreens (which types?) _____

☐ Brush Piles   ☐ Log Piles   ☐ Rock Piles/Walls   ☐ Ground Covers

☐ Meadow, Scrub or Prairie Patch   ☐ Other (Describe) _____

4. PLACES TO RAISE YOUNG

A. We provide the following for nesting birds, denning mammals, egg-laying reptiles and amphibians, fish, butterflies, and other insects and invertebrates.

☐ Mature Trees (which types?) _____

☐ Small Trees (which types?) _____

☐ Shrub Masses (which types?) _____

☐ Trees with   ☐ Dens in Ground/Rock   ☐ Wildlife Pool/Pond   ☐ Meadow, Prairie or
     Nest/Den Cavities   Scrub Patch
                                                               Size _____ sq. ft.

☐ Nesting Boxes   ☐ Nesting Shelves.
     Which animals use them? (birds, squirrels, bats, frogs, dragonflies, etc.) _____

☐ Plants for butterfly caterpillars (which types?) _____

P lease include a rough sketch or landscape diagram of your yard. If you would like, enclose some snap shots of your habitat and of you, your family or friends working in and enjoying your habitat. We cannot return the photos or sketch however, so please be sure you have duplicates for your own use.

> **Remember to submit the $15 Program Enrollment Fee (check or money order) to cover our processing and handling costs. Make check payable & send to: National Wildlife Federation, 1400 16th Street, N.W., Washington, DC 20036-2266.**

Beyond Your Certification....

The health of our environment depends on how we treat it. To get the most from your wildlife attracting efforts while practicing an environmental "good neighbor" policy in your community, try to put the landscape suggestions below into practice.

- Eliminate most turf grasses.
- Conserve water.
- Rely on natural pest control.
- Use less commercial fertilizer.
- Recycle your leaves, prunings, grass clippings, and if possible, kitchen scraps, into compost and mulches.
- Grow native plants.

For tips on how to nurture an environmentally sensible landscape, refer to NWF's Backyard Wildlife Habitat Information Packet.

Backyard Wildlife Habitats can be anywhere in your yard—front, back or all of it. If you don't have property or want to work on another habitat project, consider adopting a school, a business, a zoo, botanical garden, homeowner's common ground, natural area or nursing home. If you're involved with a habitat project in a non-traditional setting, let us hear about it. If you'd like information about a school or other community habitats, write us for an idea sheet.

To Conserve Our Natural Resources:
Printed on recycled paper containing a
minimum of 10% post consumer fiber. The
balance is pre-consumer fiber.

Plants unsuitable for wildlife gardens

Plants native to other parts of the world often find their way into our gardens because of their horticultural charm, landscape suitability, or wildlife attractiveness. Unfortunately, some of them become "invasive exotics." In the most severe cases, these plants monopolize hundreds of thousands of acres of valuable wildlife habitat, resulting in a rapid loss of diversity and stability in our natural landscapes.

When at all in doubt about how a plant that is not native to your area will act in your landscape, we encourage you to contact your state's native plant society or natural heritage program. They will tell you if the plant in question can be safely used in your area. We have included a very short list of plants which are currently causing massive problems in various parts of the United States.

Alder buckthorn (*Rhamnus frangula*)

Asian honeysuckles (*Lonicera japonica, L. maackii, L. morrowii, and L. tatarica*)

Autumn olive (*Eleagnus umbellata*)

Brazilian pepper tree (*Schinus terebinthifolius*)

Canada thistle (*Cirsium arvense*)

Crown vetch (*Coronilla varia*)

Garlic mustard (*Alliaria petiolata*)

Multiflora rose (*Rosa multiflora*)

Musk thistle (*Carduus nutans*)

Perilla or beefsteak plant (*Perilla frutescens*)

Punk tree (*Melaleuca quinquenervia*)

Purple loosestrife (*Lythrum salicaria and L. virgatum*)

Russian olive (*Elaeagnus angustifolia*)

Tamarisks or salt cedars (*Tamarix chinensis, T. ramosissima, and T. parviflora*)

Recommended reading

ADAMS, GEORGE. *Birdscaping Your Garden.* Emmaus, Pa.: Rodale Press, 1994.

Audubon Society Field Guide to North American Insects and Spiders. New York: Alfred A. Knopf, 1980.

Audubon Society Field Guide to North American Wildflowers, Eastern Region. New York: Alfred A. Knopf, 1985.

Audubon Society Field Guide to North American Wildflowers, Western Region. New York: Alfred A. Knopf, 1988.

COX, JEFF. *Landscaping with Nature.* Emmaus, Pa.: Rodale Press, 1991.

DENNIS, JOHN V. *A Complete Guide to Bird Feeding.* New York: Alfred A. Knopf, 1994.

How to Attract Hummingbirds and Butterflies. San Ramon, Ca.: Ortho Books, 1991.

IMES, RICK. *Wildflowers.* Emmaus, Pa.: Rodale Press, 1992.

KRESS, STEPHEN W. *The Audubon Society Guide to Attracting Birds.* New York: Charles Scribners Sons, 1985.

LOEWER, H. PETER. *The Wild Gardener.* Harrisburg, Pa.: Stackpole Books, 1991.

——. *The Evening Garden.* New York: Macmillan Publishing Company, 1993.

PETERSON, ROGER TORY. *A Field Guide to Birds East of the Rockies, 4th ed.* Boston: Houghton Mifflin, 1980.

——. *A Field Guide to Western Birds, 3rd ed.* Boston: Houghton Mifflin, 1990.

PROCTOR, NOBLE. *Garden Birds.* Emmaus, Pa.: Rodale Press, 1985.

——. *Song Birds.* Emmaus, Pa.: Rodale Press, 1988.

SCHNECK, MARCUS. *Butterflies.* Emmaus, Pa.: Rodale Press, 1990.

——. *Your Backyard Wildlife Garden.* Emmaus, PA: Rodale Press, 1992.

SMITH, J. ROBERT, AND BEATRICE S. SMITH. *The Prairie Garden.* Madison, Wi.: The University of Wisconsin Press, 1980.

STOKES, DONALD, AND LILLIAN STOKES. *The Hummingbird Book.* Boston: Little, Brown, & Co., 1989.

——. *The Complete Birdhouse Book.* Boston: Little, Brown, & Co., 1990.

TEKULSKY, MATTHEW. *The Butterfly Garden.* Boston: Harvard Common Press, 1985.

TUFTS, CRAIG. *The Backyard Naturalist.* Washington, D.C.: National Wildlife Federation, 1988.

Resources for wildlife gardeners

SOURCES FOR PLANTS

Grasses and Prairie Plants

Plants of the Southwest
Rte. 6, Box 11-A
Sante Fe, NM 87501
(505) 471-2212

Prairie Nursery
P.O. Box 306
Westfield, WI 53964
(608) 296-3679

Native Plants, Shrubs, and Trees

Appalachian Gardens
Box 82
Waynesboro, PA 17268
(717) 762-4312

Arrowhead Nursery
5030 Watia Rd.
Bryson City, NC 28713

Forestfarm
990 Tethercow Rd.
Williams, OR 97544
(503) 846-6963

Plants of the Wild
P.O. Box 866
Tekoa, WA 99033
(509) 284-2848

Woodlanders
1128 Colleton Ave.
Aiken, SC 29801

Perennials

Coastal Gardens & Nursery
4611 Socastee Blvd.
Myrtle Beach, SC 29575
(803) 293-2000

Holbrook Farm & Nursery
Rte. 2, Box 223 B
Fletcher, NC 28732
(704) 891-7790

Lamb Nurseries
E. 101 Sharp Ave.
Spokane, WA 99202
(509) 328-7956

Andre Viette Farm & Nursery
Rte. 1, Box 16
Fishersville, VA 22939
(703) 943-2315

Seeds

The Banana Tree
715 Northampton St.
Easton, PA 18042
(610) 253-9589

The Fragrant Path
P.O. Box 328
Ft. Calhoun, NE 68023

Chiltern Seeds
Bortree Stile, Ulverston
Cumbria LA12 7PB
England
(0229) 581137

Clyde Robin Seed Co.
P.O. Box 2855
Castro Valley, CA 94546

Plants of the Southwest
930 Baca St.
Sante Fe, NM 87501
(505) 983-1548

Water Lilies

Lilypons Water Gardens
6800 Lilypons Rd.
P.O. Box 10
Buckeystown, MD 21717
(301) 428-0686

Wildflowers

We-Du Nurseries
Rte. 5, Box 724
Marion, NC 28752
(704) 738-8300

Sunlight Gardens
174 Golden Ln.
Andersonville, TN 37705
(615) 494-8237

Niche Gardens
111 Dawson Rd.
Chapel Hill, NC 27516

Societies with Seed Exchanges

American Rock Garden Society
221 West 9th St.
Hastings, MN 55033
(612) 437-4390

Arizona Native Plant Society
P.O. Box 41206
Tuscon, AZ 85717

The Hardy Plant Society
710 Hemlock Rd.
Media, PA 19063
(215) 566-0861

Tropical Flowering Tree Society
Fairchild Tropical Garden
10901 Old Cutler Rd.
Miami, FL 33156
(305) 248-0818

CONSERVATION ORGANIZATIONS

American Bat Conservation Society
P.O. Box 1393
Rockville, MD 20849
(301) 309-6610

American Fern Society
Department of Botany
University of Tennessee
Knoxville, TN 37996-1100
(615) 974-6219

American Nature Study Society
5881 Cold Brook Rd.
Homer, NY 13077

Bat Conservation International
P.O. Box 162603
Austin, TX 78716
(512) 327-9721

Butterfly World in Florida
3600 W. Sample Rd.
Coconut Creek, FL 33073

Center for Plant Conservation
The Missouri Botanical Garden
P.O. Box 299
Saint Louis, MO 63166

Day Butterfly Center at Callaway Gardens
Highway 27
Pine Mountain, GA
1822-2000

The Nature Conservancy
1815 North Lynn St.
Arlington, VA 22209

National Audubon Society
950 Fifth Ave.
New York, NY 10022

National Wildflower Research Organization
2600 FM 973 North
Austin, TX 78725

National Wildlife Federation
1400 16th St., NW
Washington, DC
20036-2266
(202) 293-4800

New England Wild Flower Society
Hemenway Rd.
Framingham, MA 01701
(508) 877-7630

USDA plant hardiness zone map

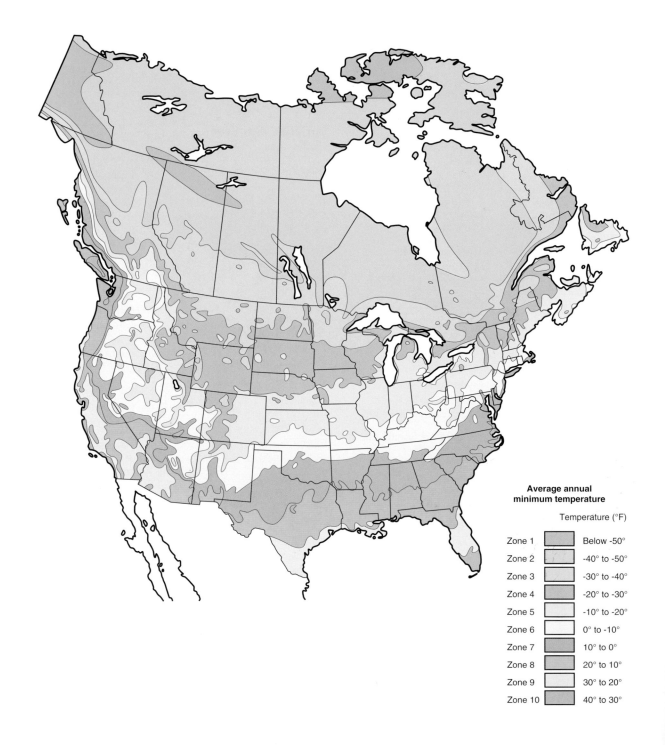

Average annual minimum temperature

Temperature (°F)

Zone 1		Below -50°
Zone 2		-40° to -50°
Zone 3		-30° to -40°
Zone 4		-20° to -30°
Zone 5		-10° to -20°
Zone 6		0° to -10°
Zone 7		10° to 0°
Zone 8		20° to 10°
Zone 9		30° to 20°
Zone 10		40° to 30°

Index

Page numbers in **boldface** indicate photos and art.

Credits

Abbreviations: T–top;
M–middle; B–bottom;
L–left; R–right

Liz Ball (PHOTO/NATS): 95
Steve Bentsen: 122B
Gay Bumgarner (PHOTO/
  NATS): 54, 85, 126, 132,
  134, 142
David Cavagnaro: 26, 29, 60,
  68, 74, 82, 90, 124, 130,
  135, 136TL, 137BL, BR,
  150, front cover M, BL
Tom Cawley: 14, 23, 39,
  79L, R, 80, 115B, 116,
  145, 146, front cover BR
Priscilla Connell (PHOTO/
NATS): 133, 137ML,
  137MR
Greg Crisei (PHOTO/NATS):
  99
Richard Day: 15, 28, 37,
  114B, 115T, 121, 137TR
Susan Day: 117, back
  cover M
David Dvorak Jr.: 57, 58L,
  59R, 66, 67, 69, 110,
  127, 137TL
Susan M. Glascock: 45, 93,
  136BL, BR, 143, 144
Dwight R. Kuhn: 13, 55,
  back cover L, front cover
  TR
Peter Loewer: 8, 140, 170,
  171L, 171R
Dorothy Long (PHOTO/
  NATS): 48
John A. Lynch (PHOTO/
  NATS): 20
Frank W. Mantlik: 59L, 63,
  104
Maslowski Wildlife
  Productions: 36, 103,
  105, 106, 107, 109, 112,
  113, front cover TL
Charles W. Melton: 70,
  114T, 122T, 129, 136TR
John F. O'Connor (PHOTO/
  NATS): 108
Jerry Pavia: 2, 10, 12, 17,
  22T, 22B, 25, 33, 34, 42,
  43, 46, 50, 52, 56, 58R,
  73, 76, 81, 89, 96, 100,
  152, 154, 155T, B, 156,
  157T, B, 158, 159L, R,
  160, 161, 162, 163L, R,
  164, 165t, L, 166, 167L,
  R, 168, 169L, R, 172,
  173L, R, 174, 175T, B,
  176, 177, 178, 179T,
  B, 180, 181L, R, 182,
  183L, R
Photo Researchers, Inc.:
  62T, B, 147
George J. Sanker (PHOTO/
  NATS): 78, back cover R
David M. Stone (PHOTO/
  NATS): 64